Joan Braune is delving into the socio-psychological roots of the fascist crisis and is helping us rebuild an empathetic, passionate, and vital social movement to protect our communities. This is an absolutely essential intervention that locates hope as a necessary weapon in the fight to stop the far right.

Shane Burley, *editor of* "No Pasaran: Antifascist Dispatches from a World in Crisis" *and author of* "Fascism Today: What It Is and How to End It"

In a political climate where fascism and the far right, once seen as historical outliers, are on the rise and becoming increasingly mainstream, the terms used for them are being problematically applied and contested, and responses to them are largely top-down, security orientated and privilege perpetrators, Joan Braune's *Understanding and Countering Fascist Movements* is a much needed intervention. The book is underpinned by philosophical insight, community engagement, activist experience, and anti-racist and anti-fascist principles and objectives. By doing so, it provides both an understanding of and response to fascism, and an important contribution to both the literature and fight. I highly recommend this book to scholars, students, and activists, as well as others trying to counter such movements.

Aaron Winter, *Senior Lecturer in Sociology (Race and Anti-Racism), Lancaster University, UK; author of* "Reactionary Democracy: How Racism and the Populist Far Right Became Mainstream" *and editor of* "Researching the Far Right: Theory, Method and Practice"

UNDERSTANDING AND COUNTERING FASCIST MOVEMENTS

This book is based on the premise that understanding fascism is crucial for defeating it.

Understanding and Countering Fascist Movements suggests fascism must be understood according to two "dimensions." First, fascism is a social movement seeking power, always already connected to sources of power. Hence, fascism cannot be defeated by policing it as a crime problem, nor therapeutically treating it as a pathology of mental health. Second, fascists have cognitive and emotional needs they are seeking to fulfill through their participation in the movement, but the presence of these motivations must be held in tension with the fact that fascists are responsible for their choices and that these individual motivations also exist in a wider social context of capitalism and systems of supremacy.

The book opens by examining some psychological elements of recruitment and disengagement from fascist movements, before addressing broader social narratives, concluding with the limitations of an approach that is grounded in the national security state that relies on individualized, perpetrator-centered interventions. Rejecting centrist paradigms that see fascism as "extremism" or "accelerationism," Braune argues that fascism must be addressed in its specificity and uniqueness as an ideology and movement. Ultimately, she argues, fascism can only be defeated by countervailing social movements that not only demand radical social change but offer alternative spaces of belonging, community care, and the search for meaning.

Understanding and Countering Fascist Movements is a philosophical contribution to antifascist theory and practice that will be appreciated by academics, students, and activists concerned about fascism today.

Joan Braune is Lecturer in Philosophy at Gonzaga University, USA. She is author and co-editor of various titles, including two books on Erich Fromm's critical theory and *The Ethics of Researching the Far Right* (forthcoming, 2024).

Routledge Studies in Fascism and the Far Right

Series editors: Nigel Copsey, Teesside University, UK and
Graham Macklin, Center for Research on Extremism (C-REX),
University of Oslo, Norway

This book series focuses upon national, transnational and global manifestations of fascist, far right and right-wing politics primarily within a historical context but also drawing on insights and approaches from other disciplinary perspectives. Its scope also includes anti-fascism, radical-right populism, extreme-right violence and terrorism, cultural manifestations of the far right, and points of convergence and exchange with the mainstream and traditional right.

Salazar
A Political Biography
Second Edition
Filipe Ribeiro de Meneses

The Italian Far Right from 1945 to the Russia-Ukraine Conflict
Nicola Guerra

Fascists in Exile
Post-War Displaced Persons in Australia
Jayne Persian

Understanding and Countering Fascist Movements
From Void to Hope
Joan Braune

For more information about this series, please visit: www.routledge.com/
Routledge-Studies-in-Fascism-and-the-Far-Right/book-series/FFR

UNDERSTANDING AND COUNTERING FASCIST MOVEMENTS

From Void to Hope

Joan Braune

Routledge
Taylor & Francis Group

LONDON AND NEW YORK

Designed cover image: © Getty Images

First published 2024
by Routledge
4 Park Square, Milton Park, Abingdon, Oxon OX14 4RN

and by Routledge
605 Third Avenue, New York, NY 10158

Routledge is an imprint of the Taylor & Francis Group, an informa business

British Library Cataloguing-in-Publication Data
A catalogue record for this book is available from the British Library

Library of Congress Cataloging-in-Publication Data
Names: Braune, Joan, author.
Title: Understanding and countering fascist movements : from void to hope / Joan Braune.
Description: Abingdon, Oxon ; New York, NY : Routledge, 2024. |
Series: Fascism and the far right | Includes bibliographical references and index.
Identifiers: LCCN 2023037549 (print) | LCCN 2023037550 (ebook) | ISBN 9780367468699 (hardback) | ISBN 9780367696986 (paperback) | ISBN 9781003031604 (ebook)
Subjects: LCSH: Fascism—Social aspects. | Fascism—Psychological aspects. | Anti-fascist movements. | Social change.
Classification: LCC JC481 .B694 2024 (print) | LCC JC481 (ebook) | DDC 320.53/3—dc23/eng/20230909
LC record available at https://lccn.loc.gov/2023037549
LC ebook record available at https://lccn.loc.gov/2023037550

ISBN: 978-0-367-46869-9 (hbk)
ISBN: 978-0-367-69698-6 (pbk)
ISBN: 978-1-003-03160-4 (ebk)

DOI: 10.4324/9781003031604

Typeset in Sabon
by codeMantra

CONTENTS

ACKNOWLEDGMENTS

In many ways, large and small, so many people have sustained me in mind, heart, and spirit over the past several years, culminating in this book. It is impossible to name them all. Even though this topic has required looking at some painful content, I have also been transformed by encountering the strategic activism, insightful research, and courageous truth-telling of so many people, including many people who have done work in this or related areas for far longer than I have. If you have offered me guidance or encouragement in this work at any time, please know that I am deeply grateful.

Without implying agreement with any of my claims, I would like to thank Helmut-Harry Loewen and Aaron Winter for their feedback on one of the chapters, and Jordan Denari Duffner for feedback on a related topic. Likewise, for interviews and dialogue that helped me approach some issues related to formers and/or recent white nationalist movements, I would like to thank Katie McHugh and two formers whom I do not have permission to name.

My friend and fellow Critical Theorist countering fascism, Claudia Leeb, helped me stay on track and complete publication of the book through our years of writing accountability meetings in which we encouraged one another on our projects and set goals. My parents, Nick and Linda Braune, have been a steady source of inspiration and emotional support and provided feedback on some drafts. My fellow activist-organizer/researcher friends, Kate Bitz and Eric Warwick, have kept me going as we have swapped insights and news on the rising fascist threat over the years and collaborated on some projects, and while I did not ask them for help reading drafts of this book, I can feel their influence in how I approached certain topics. My thanks and gratitude to you all.

In addition, I am grateful to the Gonzaga Center for the Study of Hate (formerly Gonzaga Institute for Hate Studies) and especially the recent Director, Kristine Hoover. Through the Center, I have been able to grow in my scholarship and learn from other researchers by participating in the Center's international conferences and journal. For over 25 years, since the period of the Aryan Nations compound in North Idaho, Gonzaga University has housed a center devoted to studying and countering hate and othering; due to recent funding decisions, the Center may be restructuring or seeking a new institutional home, but I remain hopeful about new directions the work might take and am deeply grateful for the productive work it has made possible and to Kristine for her leadership and guidance.

This is not a very long book, but in some ways, I have been writing it for about six years while doing other projects in between. The book was born out of heartbreak and began with a story I do not have permission to tell, as I witnessed firsthand the hurt and harm caused by white supremacist movements, impacting families and children in lasting ways. It would feel presumptuous to dedicate the book to those harmed by that horrible situation, but I cannot close the book without taking a moment to bear witness to the toll these movements take on whole communities. As we remember the harm and loss of the past, we continue the fight against fascism and for communities that welcome our search for meaning, justice, and peace.

INTRODUCTION

Fascism is many things: mobilized hate and violence; a defense system for white supremacy; an attempt on the part of the capitalist ruling class to maintain power; a defense of racism, misogyny, homophobia and transphobia, xenophobia, ableism, and other oppressions. It is also *a false solution to a quest for meaning*.

The sense of urgency and desperation to find an answer to the question of human meaning that so many feel today is exacerbated by capitalism. Theoretically shallow but psychologically tangled, fascism's core message is that injustice is rampant and invincible and that you should choose to be on the winning team, restoring your kind to power by trampling the weaker ones, those destined to lose.

If we wish to fight fascism, we must understand it. (Erich Fromm, whom I will say more about later, wrote this deceptively obvious statement in 1941.) This book is a contribution to understanding contemporary fascist movements, particularly in the United States, in order to defeat them. This task of understanding is a collective one, requiring the perspectives and voices of many, especially those long marginalized by oppressive power structures and long targeted by hate. The project I undertake here is only a very small piece of a much larger collective undertaking. Although I have a half-Jewish background and have experienced fear and trauma due to antisemitism and my work against hate, I also know that I have not suffered nearly as much as so many others and that, in general, as I walk through the world as a white, straight, middle-income, able-bodied cis woman, I do not often find myself at the "sharp end of the stick" of fascist hate.

Because my mind is particularly occupied with and troubled by the recruitment of young people into hate movements, something I have witnessed up

DOI: 10.4324/9781003031604-1

close in my community through to its devastating consequences, I explore the *pull* of fascism—the ways in which fascist movements play upon deep human desires and twist and manipulate their recruits' search for meaning into a violent defense of ideological idols. Fascism promises to fill profound voids in human beings, but the promise it offers proves false. We must understand the nature and content of this promise if we wish to effectively counteract its pull.

Seeking understanding of how capitalist alienation and fascist recruitment tactics coalesce to build new hate-filled movements is an antifascist practice, not a naïve appeal for kindness to fascists. Fascists are dangerous; they are morally responsible for their choices, and communities must work to shut down fascist organizing by establishing clear boundaries, ostracizing fascists from public spaces, and depriving them of platforms to spew hate. Any space in which fascists feel included and able to express their views is a space in which their targets are not safe and are not included. Fascism must be understood in order to be defeated, but it must be defeated by social movements that fight back against fascism and demand far more than the end of fascism but rather the liberation of all humanity.

Fascism must be understood on two levels. First, it is a social movement seeking power,[1] always already connected to sources of power. Second, it is composed of individuals, whose pathways into organized hate and violent authoritarianism differ but that often follow familiar patterns, including an attempt to meet certain emotional and psychological needs through participation in the fascist movement. The basic premise of this book is that strategies for fighting fascism often break down by excluding one or the other of these two dimensions (the social movement dimension and the individual psychological dimension), and that part of the contribution that scholars can make, perhaps especially those of us trained in the interdisciplinary Marxist tradition of Critical Theory, which provides the foundation of modern theories of the authoritarian personality in relation to fascist ideology, is to clarify each of these dimensions and bring into clarity the interaction and interdependence of these two dimensions. Always in the background of my investigation into these themes is not only my training in Critical Theory as a particular school and method of thought but also my more general training as an academic philosopher and my experience as an activist in my community confronting fascist movements in the Pacific Northwest.

As a philosopher, my method here engages questions of human meaning and focuses less on historical details, on explications of differing fascist organizations, and attempts to empirically quantify the rise in hate group recruitment and hate crime. Although this book is not an introductory explainer on the landscape of contemporary fascist movements, I hope it can still be fruitfully engaged by some non-academics and that what I offer will be useful, especially to my context in the United States. The method here is philosophical, at times existentialist, especially in the first two chapters, as I attempt to understand the sources of fascist ideology, as it seeks to fill voids of meaning with apocalyptic narratives and myths. As an activist, I am also attuned throughout the book to the ways in which approaches that might seem appealing to grant agencies and mainstream media outlets, which suggest mod and innovative new categories of analysis to describe current trends in far-right mobilization—"coalitional accelerationism," "cumulative extremism," "reciprocal radicalization," and so forth—and which argue for responses grounded in policing and securitization, run afield of the grassroots needs of communities on the front lines of antifascist struggle. Instead, I suggest that a continuity of present antifascist struggle and analysis with past traditions of analysis and praxis is not only possible but also necessary, and "fascism" remains a category of enduring importance and continuity. I also hope that my position as both a philosopher and an activist provides a useful standpoint from which to contribute to an understanding of fascism in its dual dimensions.

A myopic focus on either of the two dimensions of fascism—the social movement dimension and the individual psychological dimension—gives rise to misunderstandings that pose problems for effectively combating and eradicating the threat of fascist movements. The social movement standpoint is prone to excessive suspicion of psychological investigation, worrying that too much interest in what attracts people to fascism will result in a form of empathy that betrays solidarity with fascism's victims. While caution is necessary and concerns about the risks of empathy must be expressed and discussed, understanding how fascism attracts and how it recruits can be a contribution to a project of solidarity and emancipation aimed at the defeat of fascism. A perspective that sees fascism solely as a social movement to be outnumbered and crushed in the streets may fail to understand how the psychological appeal of fascist movements arises (under certain social conditions) and may also be lacking in certain types of knowledge that could help to prevent and counter recruitment while simultaneously maintaining an activist perspective and rejecting reliance on policing and state securitization.

The standpoint that focuses exclusively on the individualized psychological dimension, however, tends to miss the ways in which fascism is always already partly *normal*, resting on structures, systems, and the normalization of racism in society, as well as capitalism and other systems of oppression, including misogyny, homophobia, transphobia, nativism, antisemitism, Islamophobia, and ableism. The individualized dimension tends to focus on factors that may make some individuals more vulnerable to fascist recruitment, such as trauma and social isolation. This focus underestimates the ways in which fascism can be to the selfish advantage of participants, who are not universally miserable and struggling. Especially as these movements are currently resurgent and more publicly allied to or adjacent to political power, young people who join fascist movements may reasonably be imagining a bright future working for a senator or writing for a right-wing news outlet rather than reacting to trauma in a near-suicidal manner and envisioning themselves to be signing up for either future imprisonment or death in a coming "race war." Although alienation or dissatisfaction of some kind may still be present amid the excitement of a path to power, too much emphasis on fascism as "extreme" or on fascists as traumatized and lonely can make us look for it in the wrong places and miss it when it shows up with greater adjacency to power.

Structure of the Book

The first chapter of this book undertakes a philosophical, existentialist, and Critical Theory exploration of the psychological appeal of fascism today, focusing on how fascism recruits by promising to fill a void of meaning that exists in all human beings and that is exacerbated by capitalism. Fascism provides a false and unstable answer to the question of meaning and identity, creating a shallow sense of self that can only be maintained and defended through escalating violence. In the second chapter, I explore the role of myths of destruction and rebirth in fascism and fascism's belief that history moves in cycles. The fascist imagines that they are to play the role of "hero" in destroying the world so that it can be born again, completing the next stage of the cycle. Fascism is "accelerationist," in the sense that it believes destruction must be accelerated in order for the world to reset itself back to the hierarchical vision fascists defend. I explore the term "accelerationism" further, outlining some of the ways its meaning is being expanded, and I believe misapplied, by some in the counterterrorism field.

The third chapter explores former Trump advisor and far-right mobilizer Steve Bannon's apocalyptic vision, demonstrating in the process that a politics of destructive accelerationism is not merely a fringe criminal phenomenon that can be overcome through moving people to the political center and rejecting "polarization." Rather, apocalyptic visions of destruction and rebirth also show up at centers of power. I explore Bannon's rise to power, his ideology, and his frequent "signaling" of affinities with fascists.

The fourth and final chapter critiques mainline "counter-extremism" and "deradicalization" approaches to fighting hate, which tend to frame the problem as being one of "polarization" and "extremism" and which wrongly suggest that centrism and the status quo are the site of safety and the source of the solution to fascist violence. These counter-extremism approaches, as seen, for example, in "Countering Violent Extremism" programs that have engaged in profiling of Muslim communities and surveillance of the left, are damaging, undermining work for social, racial, and economic justice, and relying on a discourse that empowers the right. These ideas also shape the narratives that become most dominant in the counter-extremism industry, including a problematic "compassion narrative" that claims fascists can be deradicalized through kind outreach from members of targeted groups.

A critique of these institutions, practices, and discourses can be undertaken while still holding the insights obtained from a psychological and philosophical investigation of how fascist recruitment offers to fill voids. Although the centrist counter-extremism milieu tends to rely on psychological investigation to the exclusion of political and social critique, some insights obtained from this work can still be applied in left, antifascist struggle that simultaneously acknowledges the ways in which fascism is a social movement seeking power, always already connected to sources of power.

Definitions of Fascism

The debate about how to define fascism is highly fraught, and although this small book does intervene in certain ways into that discussion, it is not my objective to introduce or defend a single definition of fascism. I do begin from the following premises:

1 Fascism is a political and philosophical category, referring both to an ideology and to a social movement in favor of that ideology. (I say more about definitions of "ideology" in Chapter 2.) "Fascism" is also a term used to describe states, but I will not be exploring here the question of whether the United States, or other countries, should be designated as fully "fascist," as opposed to merely containing various fascist elements, including at the institutional level.

2 Fascism is a right-wing political movement, though not all right-wing movements are fascist. Fascism often appropriates ideas from the left or seeks to infiltrate or build temporary coalitions with sections of the left,[2] but it is an inherently right-wing movement, and leftists are always among its primary targets and victims.

3 Fascism is not just a word for things one does not like. Although fascism is violent, cruel, and authoritarian, not everything that is violent, cruel, or authoritarian is "fascist." The point of saying this is not to police language but to clarify categories. A protester who screams, "Fascists!" in front of a Border Patrol office is not "wrong"—it is safe to assume that the protester is not making a narrow analytical claim that those specific Border Patrol officers in that office are sitting around reading *Mein Kampf* at night (although I am sure there *are* Border Patrol officers who are reading *Mein Kampf*). Rather, the protester is speaking out against the fascistic behavior of the Border Patrol—whether or not an individual Border Patrol officer has joined a fascist movement or is actively engaging with fascist ideology, they play a role in the work of fascism, by excluding and brutalizing

non-white people seeking to enter the country. However, in speaking of fascists in this book, I am not speaking simply of fascistic behavior but of a social movement. Understanding this social movement provides insights for defeating it and for reducing fascistic behavior and policies in society at large.

4 Fascism is not equivalent to censorship of speech, vaccine mandates, government surveillance, or unchecked corporate power. On the last point, particularly, although fascism seems only to arise as a political option under capitalism and does play a role in shoring up capitalism by transmuting anger at the rich into anger at scapegoated groups, there is more to fascism than capitalist markets. People often quote Mussolini out of context, referring to his calling fascism "corporatism," and point to this as an indication that unchecked corporate power is the same as fascism, but "corporatism" as referenced by Mussolini and the Italian fascists referred to a specific antidemocratic political philosophy, and it was not about claiming that Wal-Mart or Amazon should be regulated less or pay less taxes.

Definitions of fascism vary, fluctuating between emphasizing psychological, ideological, or structural and economic aspects.[3] Some of the most respected work on fascism within political science has been done by Robert O. Paxton and Roger Griffin. Paxton's detailed definition of fascism focuses on fascism's ideological beliefs rather than its economic function:

> Fascism may be defined as a form of political behavior marked by obsessive preoccupation with community decline, humiliation, or victimhood and by compensatory cults of unity, energy, and purity, in which a mass-based party of committed nationalist militants, working in uneasy but effective collaboration with traditional elites, abandons democratic liberties and pursues with redemptive violence and without ethical or legal restraints goals of internal cleansing and external expansion.[4]

(Paxton also famously describes a series of stages, through which fascists come to power, but, again, my focus here is less the question of whether my country, the United States, or some other country, is or is becoming a "fascist state" and more on the nature of social movements that wish it to be so.) Roger Griffin, with a similar emphasis on ideology, stressed fascism's "palingenetic ultranationalism."[5] Palingenesis means "rebirth." I talk further in Chapter 2 about how fascism relies on a cyclical vision of history, involving destruction and rebirth.

Fascism is hard to define partly due to the nature of its own beliefs. Fascism largely rejects reason and believes truth is a product of power and violence, as opposed to something to be uncovered or revealed. I am tempted to agree with the statement of Jose Carlos Mariátegui that fascism is "not a concept."[6] In other words, fascism's ideological content is not rationally defined, and fascism is motivated in many ways by irrational forces. At the same time, fascism can serve the rational self-interest of the capitalist class and often does–witness, for example, the fearmongering about "Critical Race Theory" going on right now with the help of Koch brothers' funded think tanks[7] that combat anti-racist education in schools and open up more space for fascist resurgence and recruitment.

In lieu of a lexical definition, fascism may need to be defined by what philosopher Ludwig Wittgenstein called "family resemblances"; in fact, Umberto Eco suggests as much in his famous essay on "ur-fascism."[8] One might point to a list of characteristics, such as racist and sexist prejudices, conspiracy theories, scapegoating, genocidal ambitions, an emphasis on an "us" and a "them," a cult of violence, authoritarianism, the privileging of a "movement" or "people" over the rule of law, nostalgia for a past social order, apocalyptic visions of the future destruction of the present social order, the use of armed paramilitary forces, and the belief that a natural hierarchy has been upended and must be restored. How many elements may need to be present for something to be "fascist," may be unclear, but a "laundry list" approach gets us to a level of familiarity with the concept.

Radical Alternatives and the Importance of Left Solidarity

Defeating fascism requires mass movements. The left must also build structures that can pull people away from fascism, preferring to counter-recruit than to meet fascism in the street when the former is an option. We need to build radical left alternatives that provide not only a more coherent narrative but also sources of meaning and community that provide more stable solutions to the void that fascism seeks to fill. This is achieved not through naïve attempts at outreach that fail to account for fascists' danger to the public but through the construction of alternative social structures. The far-right in Europe is reading the leftist Antonio Gramsci and appropriating long-held leftist practices of dual power support structures (like free clinics) and mutual aid (like food drives), and the U.S. far-right has copy-catted some of these attempts although generally on a much smaller scale. Although the right is doing this mainly tactically and for show—not with the concern for universal human care that undergirds real left commitments—this constitutes a warning to be alert and for the left to strengthen its own tools of outreach, support, and alternative structures. We can learn from past left efforts, such as the unemployed councils of the Communist Party in the 1930s, the free breakfast program of the Black Panthers in the 1960s, and the more recent humanitarian outreach of Occupy Wall Street after Hurricane Sandy, members of Democratic Socialists of America providing "free brake light checks," or antifascists helping those impacted by recent wildfires in the Pacific Northwest. Projects of mutual aid and dual power help to organize, to demonstrate our values, and to begin now to construct the new world we desire. They also provide those desperate for help a way forward, a form of social support that does not lead down conspiracy theory rabbit holes, and an alternative to seeking solace on the far-right.

Over the past ten years, there have been rebellious shifts away from politics as usual around the world, and these shifts have sometimes taken a right-wing and nationalistic form. The reasons for this are partly economic, but the voters who have shifted to the right are not at the bottom of the economic pyramid[9]—instead, they are responding to a sense of instability, malaise, and aggrievement that has a variety of causes, including alienation under capitalism. As the left attempts to rekindle working-class solidarity against the capitalist class, the right turns to nationalism against the "globalist" power structures. As always, the right attempts to shift attention to scapegoats, identifying minority groups or foreign influences as "corrupting" capitalism rather than rooting the problem in capitalism itself.

The far-right is not a product of a working-class revolt; after all, the far-right has powerful and wealthy backers, without which its influence would be hard to imagine. As the stability of mainstream politics is threatened by its lack of commitment to working people and inability to deal with economic crisis, in the absence of a well-organized left, some people will seek solace on the far-right, which appeals to their hopelessness and malaise. As people despair of political futures, conspiracy theories can easily fill a political void and provide a sense of community and meaning lacking in alienated contemporary society.

This is not to say that a "class reductionist" analysis of fascism is acceptable, seeing fascism only as a product of misdirected anger by oppressed workers and ignoring the role of racism and other oppressions. Fascism arises specifically under capitalism, and ultimately the threat of fascism cannot be defeated, in my view, without the defeat of capitalism. However, struggles against capitalism must include and intersect with struggles against structures of oppression and violence against people of color, including Black and indigenous people in the United States and others, as well as against women, sexual and gender minorities, Jews, Muslims, those with disabilities, and others. We are also in an "all hands on deck" situation in the United States—anticapitalism or a leftist identity is not a prerequisite for participating in work against fascism and hate, but seeing the ways in which fascism is related to capitalism will be necessary for the ultimate defeat of the fascist threat.

It is my earnest hope that this book—a focused intervention into current discussions and debates about fascism and how to defeat it—will assist both scholars and communities in thinking critically about how fascism recruits, its adjacency to power, and the reasons why we must respond with social movements instead of relying on state-sponsored counter-extremism programs, policing, or mere rhetorical appeals to kindness and dialogue.

Notes

1 I am indebted for this important phrase to a conversation with Cristien Storm, who addresses the need for boundaries with the white nationalist movement in her book: *Empowered Boundaries: Speaking Truth, Setting Boundaries, and Inspiring Social Change* (Berkeley, CA: North Atlantic Books, 2018).
2 Alexander Reid Ross, *Against the Fascist Creep* (Chico: AK Press, 2017), 3.
3 Dave Renton, *Fascism: Theory and Practice* (London: Pluto Press, 1999), 18.
4 Robert Paxton, *The Anatomy of Fascism* (New York: Vintage Books, 2005), 218.
5 Roger Griffin, *The Nature of Fascism* (London: Routledge, 1993), 39.
6 Federico Finchelstein, *A Brief History of Fascist Lies* (Oakland: University of California Press, 2020), 56.
7 Ralph Wilson and Isaac Kamola. *Free Speech and Koch Money: Manufacturing a Campus Culture War* (London: Pluto Press, 2021), 156.
8 Umberto Eco, "Ur-Fascism," *The New York Review of Books*, June 22, 1995, https://www.pegc.us/archive/Articles/eco_ur-fascism.pdf.
9 Aurelien Mondon and Aaron Winter, *Reactionary Democracy: How Racism and the Populist Far Right Became Mainstream* (London: Verso, 2020).

Bibliography

Burley, Shane. *Fascism Today: What It Is and How to End It*. Chico: AK Press, 2017.

Eco, Umberto. "Ur-Fascism." *The New York Review of Books*, June 22, 1995. https://www.pegc.us/archive/Articles/eco_ur-fascism.pdf.

Finchelstein, Federico. *A Brief History of Fascist Lies*. Oakland: University of California Press, 2020.

Griffin, Roger. *The Nature of Fascism*. London: Routledge, 1993.

Mondon, Aurelien and Aaron Winter. *Reactionary Democracy: How Racism and the Populist Far Right Became Mainstream*. London: Verso, 2020.

Paxton, Robert. *The Anatomy of Fascism*. New York: Vintage Books, 2005.

Renton, Dave. *Fascism: Theory and Practice*. London: Pluto Press, 1999.

Ross, Alexander Reid. *Against the Fascist Creep*. Chico: AK Press, 2017.

Storm, Cristien. *Empowered Boundaries: Speaking Truth, Setting Boundaries, and Inspiring Social Change*. Berkeley, CA: North Atlantic Books, 2018.

Wilson, Ralph and Isaac Kamola. *Free Speech and Koch Money: Manufacturing a Campus Culture War*. London: Pluto Press, 2021.

1

VOID AND IDOL

Although *fascism is a social movement seeking power, always already connected to sources of power*, it is also composed of individuals who have a variety of psychological, ideological, and situational reasons for participating in it. This chapter explores the latter aspect of fascism, looking at how a driving factor in fascist recruitment, both past and present, is an attempt to fill a "void" of meaning that the individual experiences both in their own life and in society at large. I show some of the ways that this theme arises in the discourse of current and former fascists, as well as how it was philosophically explored by critics of fascism, especially the philosophers Erich Fromm and Simone Weil, who independently formulated highly similar critiques of fascism. Both Fromm and Weil pointed to the concept of a void; the role of "idolatry" or "ideology" in filling personal voids with a temporary, unstable sense of personal identity and purpose; and how that fragile sense of identity and purpose is then defended and enforced with increasing levels of destructiveness and violence. Understanding how this void operates is crucial for understanding how to counteract fascist recruitment and advances a radical critique of societies that continue to give rise to fascist movements.

This chapter explores some psychological, individual factors that lead individuals to join fascist movements, from a philosophical perspective. Such an inquiry into the psychology of individual fascists can be distressing. One reason for this discomfort is that such an exploration must use what one might call a kind of *strategic empathy*, i.e., an intellectual curiosity about fascists' experiences and motivations that analyzes them as persons like ourselves who are choosing an incorrect (and immoral) means of filling certain human needs that are nonetheless rooted in the general human condition and

DOI: 10.4324/9781003031604-2

the social conditions of the societies we all inhabit.[1] Although this strategic empathy can feel in dissonance with the knowledge of the incalculable harm fascists do and have done, understanding the psychological mechanisms that contribute to individuals' involvement in fascist movements is very different from excusing their actions. No one—and especially not victims or likely targets of fascists—is obliged to empathize with, feel sorry for, or forgive fascists; in fact, such demands made on victims and targets can create cycles of abuse and harm. Nor should this exercise in strategic empathy, in pursuit of understanding certain aspects of fascism, be confused with encouragement to show fascists kindness in the hope it will change their views. I cannot even begin to emphasize enough that fascists are dangerous, and boundaries that keep communities safe must always be prioritized over any kind of outreach.[2] (In my public and community educational work against hate groups, I some-times feel I spend a good 80% of the time convincing well-meaning white liberals not to go have a beer with the Proud Boys to overcome "polariza-tion" or "iron out their differences." As I will explain further in Chapter 4, rhetorical appeals to compassionate outreach to fascists can have numerous harmful effects despite some of the potentially heartwarming stories members of the public have heard about people who allegedly left hate groups by mak-ing new friends.) I also want to caution that this chapter should not be read as advice on how to disengage or "deradicalize" friends or family members who have gotten involved in fascist movements; I am not an expert or a prac-titioner in that area.

Much of the core argument of this chapter was written in 2017–2018 and was developed into an article that was published in the *Journal of Hate Studies*.[3] Since that time, my thinking on these topics has developed considerably. I have taken care here to modify as necessary. I am a philoso-pher, an activist, and a teacher. Although I am writing in this chapter partly about matters that concern "deradicalization" practitioners, I am doing so as a philosopher, drawing on Critical Theoretical and spiritual-existentialist frameworks. Beginning in Chapter 2, I develop a critique of the mainline counterterrorism/counter-extremism industry's model for analyzing fascism and the far-right, and I continue this critique at greater length in Chapter 4, but I begin here with the elements of the psychological/existentialist explora-tion I have so far undertaken and that I continue to find useful.

Ultimately I have chosen to include this chapter because I believe it is helpful in two respects: (1) for thinking about methods of counter-recruiting people, especially young people, from the far-right and (2) for thinking about left strategy in the long term for the defeat of fascism, including the need to build structures within the present that give space to culture, commu-nity, dialogue, and philosophical questioning and that challenge capitalist alienation. I hope that this chapter provides fruitful reflection for academ-ics, practitioners, community activists, and others, on how to approach the deep, existential questions to which fascism provides a twisted and ultimately unsatisfying answer that is anti-rational and rooted in cruelty and that can only ever be enforced and defended by means of violence.

The Void

The theme of a "void"—or language evoking other kinds of holes or absences, such as "abyss," "rabbit hole," "emptiness," "chasm," "vacuum," "black hole," and "pothole"—runs through the literature on fascism and the far-right like a red thread. Political scientists might say that fascism is made possible by *political voids:* as mainstream political parties fail to address the needs of the citizenry through mainstream political institutions, fascist parties and movements capitalize on discontent by directing the populace's anger at scapegoated minorities. More psychological frames of analysis emphasize the attraction of fascism for individuals experiencing personal voids, depression, traumas, and life events like "potholes,"[4] which throw the individual off course. Journalists and public commentators alike describe the descent into fascism in terms that similarly evoke absences or holes: as going down "rabbit holes," being sucked into a void, encountering darkness, or "going to the dark side." Furthermore, the reemergence out of the dark cave of fascism into the metaphorical light of day is often described, sometimes by former fascists themselves, as finding the courage to face voids, to die (metaphorically), to jump off cliffs, or to enter an abyss or vacuum of meaning, and the period of time after leaving hate before reconnecting to our shared humanity is often described as journeying through a kind of void, vacuum, or abyss.

Anyone leaving one identity without yet having another passes through a "vacuum" experience,[5] writes Helen Fuchs Ebaugh, a sociologist and former Catholic nun who wrote a study of "role exits," such as nuns leaving a convent, women giving up children to a partner in a divorce, and individuals transitioning to a new gender identity. For those leaving fascism, a "role exit" she does not directly address, the "vacuum experience" is further complicated by fascism's own undermining of reason and meaning in favor of power and violence. In fascism's view, truth lies in internally felt and chosen myth (however much that myth may be artificially fabricated), which fascism then attempts to force into reality through violence.[6] This means that abandoning fascism requires obtaining not only a new *source* of meaning but also a new *relationship* to questions of meaning. Exit from fascism also, unlike certain other role exits, requires grappling with the shame of having done harm as part of one's prior identity.

The appeal of fascism for those who join it depends heavily on fascism's promise to fill a void of meaning. Rather than confronting voids of meaning honestly, however, fascism blames a scapegoated "other" for these voids: Blacks or other people of color, Jews, Muslims, LGBTQ+ individuals, feminists, Marxists, and so on. In fascism's view, the "other" has "taken" the meaning that ought to be present and has caused this gaping absence of wholeness. Fascism then directs the alienated individual's rage toward this other. But rage against scapegoats, and the accompanying ideological idols that prop up that rage, only temporarily plugs the void of meaning in the individual. Fascist ideology provides an unstable new sense of personal identity and a "great cause" to fanatically defend. Angry young people or others desperately searching for meaning find only temporary relief through this hate-filled ideology.

I argue that the path away from fascism, whether avoiding its appeal in the first place or leaving the fascist movement after having joined it, therefore requires facing the reality of the void and consciously passing through the void. This means encountering a lack of meaning and not fleeing it but working through it with courage and a kind of philosophical honesty about the ways in which life provides questions that do not come with simplistic answers attached yet also with the knowledge and hope that growth in wisdom and insight is possible, requiring patience, openness, dialogue with others, and attention to reality as it is, not as one wishes it to be. Passing through this void is not merely a matter of individual emotional toughness nor an automatic process—it requires the individual rethinking and reworking her relationship to identity itself, which is a philosophical question, not merely a task to be undertaken therapeutically. An honest confrontation with the experience of a "void" might also result in the discovery that some feelings of alienation experienced by the individual were caused by social injustices that the individual had not correctly identified and that may only ultimately be changed through movements for social change, but the question of the individual's sense of identity cannot be bypassed by the individual turning immediately to political involvement, since this could simply create a new false solution to the void.

Beyond Identity Replacement

The inquiry I am undertaking both builds upon and critiques the reigning wisdom of "counter-extremism" and "deradicalization" academics and professionals, who see identity formation as a crucial factor in recruitment to "extremism."[7] A related piece of accepted wisdom, coming out of the work of Norwegian social scientist Tore Bjørgo, is that extremists join their movements in pursuit of a sense of group belonging.[8] These claims are encapsulated in one of the founding documents of "deradicalization" work in the United States, produced by the 2011 Google Ideas conference, which states that individuals drawn into "violent extremism" are motivated not primarily by ideology but by needs for "a sense of belonging, an identity, and a sense of purpose."[9]

The apparent importance of a search for identity might suggest that the challenge lies in finding a "new identity" for the extremist,[10] such as through a tie to a romantic partner or children who the individual believes can be better served without their involvement in the movement.[11] Sometimes the new identity encouraged might be more specific—carpenter, church-goer, captain of the soccer team—or found in broader concepts such as law-abiding loyalty to the nation-state. In some cases, people adopt a new identity as a "former extremist" who works with other "formers" to counter the movements they once participated in.

Although it is true that "identity" is one of the appeals of fascist movements for those who join them, this chapter is also a caution against replacing that identity too quickly with a new one. The problem is not just that youth or others who join fascist movements have chosen a fascist identity and need to be given another, more positive identity. Rather, their *relationship* to identity is flawed and needs to be reworked before they adopt a new identity. They joined these movements not only because they chose an incorrect identity but because they had a flawed understanding of what identity is, what it offers to an individual, and how one arrives at a sense of personal identity in relationship to one's life trajectory (or narrative) as well as one's various facets of group belonging. I will show, for example, that replacing "extremist" identity with national identity reifies identity, making it an "idol," and can lead to other harms. Instead of replacing one identity with a new identity, I propose that academics, practitioners, and activists concerned with prevention or counter-recruitment undertake further study of the question: *How do we lead people to the patience that waits for truth, that is open and imagines differently?* Such openness and imagination are prerequisites for a more emancipatory politics that challenges the conditions that make fascism possible through a critique of all idols including national identity and all forms of authoritarian idolatry. Hence, identity is part of the issue, but the challenge is not primarily that of acquiring a "new identity" but a new way of encountering identity, not as something to be grasped but in fact as something primarily to be released.

A "search for identity" may not be the only, primary, or distinguishing factor of involvement in fascist movements. In fact, this would not help in providing a profile for spotting potential "extremists" (and profiles of potential "extremists" should be avoided anyway).[12] In fact, *all or most* young people are searching for an identity, and human beings of all ages are constantly reorienting themselves, seeking their place in the world and defining their lives narratively, philosophically, and existentially. Joining fascist movements is a choice of a *particular* identity, not just *any* identity. However, as I will show, fascism offers to fill voids of identity and meaning in a very specific way, which must be understood in order to be countered.

The ways in which fascism may be bound up with questions of self, truth, and meaning suggest a need for philosophers to be engaged in the work of understanding and countering fascist recruitment and rethinking processes of disengagement from fascism. These are philosophical questions and the province of the Humanities. These are questions not only for psychologists but for philosophers as well; they are questions that dialogue and dialectics can undertake in pursuit of truth, not only matters for emotional processing and coping. In fact, though I cannot prove it, I suspect that philosophical study and philosophical conversation with youth might help avert fascist recruitment before they join or help those who are consciously leaving fascism to rethink their beliefs. This is not a task to be undertaken lightly, however, nor by individuals working alone—the safety and agency of targets must be prioritized over any form of prevention or reintegration, and many people underestimate the danger fascists pose and the depth of the harm they inflict. However, countering fascism is in part of a philosophical task, as fascism is, among other things, a belief system, and fascists not only engage in harmful behavior but also immerse themselves in a worldview, in some cases involving extensive reading and study of texts or mass consumption of lectures and political material online. Countering or unwinding fascism's claims would involve not only therapy but also thinking critically about what one believes to be true about one's self and the world and reflecting upon how truth about such matters is to be obtained.

Simone Weil and Erich Fromm were philosophers with a particular account of how we approach questions of identity and how filling voids of identity with "idols" like fascism can give rise to violence. I will first outline some of the overlapping concerns of Weil and Fromm, and then we shall see how similar claims are backed up by the rhetoric and discourses of fascists and former fascists today.

Simone Weil and Erich Fromm on the "Void"

The theme of the "void" plays a role in the work of Erich Fromm (1900–1980) and Simone Weil (1909–1943). Both Fromm and Weil were leftist twentieth-century philosophers and social critics of Jewish descent, yet their methods and approaches differed greatly. The Marxist Critical Theorist Fromm and the Christian mystic Weil can explain today's resurgent fascist movements, through their peculiar synchronicities on the topics of the void, ideology or idolatry as ways of filling the void, and destructiveness as the violent defense of idols or ideology.

Fromm and Weil independently developed a highly similar analysis of fascism and the void. Although the term "void" does not feature prominently in Fromm's writing as it does in Weil's, Fromm's theory of fascism as an "escape from freedom" turns on the same notion of fascism as an attempt to fill a void of meaning. Moreover, both Fromm and Weil use the terms "idolatry" and "destruction" (or "destructiveness") to describe the means by which fascism stuffs voids with simplistic ideologies and then defends (or enforces) those ideologies with violence and cruelty. Both Weil and Fromm—and I agree with them on this—see fascism as a failed attempt to fill the void in advance of facing the reality of the void (a very real absence or crisis of meaning). The only way out (not only for individuals leaving hate groups but perhaps also for societies seeking to overcome fascism's threat) is to face the void one initially sought to flee. This initial "void" is in some sense grounded in the human condition itself, but it manifests itself in a particular way in contemporary late capitalism that, converging with certain individual psychological factors, motivates certain individuals to evade it by means of fascism specifically.

Erich Fromm, Alienation, and Mechanisms of Escape

Understanding the void requires engaging the Frankfurt School's work on authoritarianism, especially with regard to Fromm's work on authoritarianism and its relationship to alienation and rebellion. When Erich Fromm was recruited to join the Frankfurt Institute for Social Research, then director Max Horkheimer tasked Fromm with a project in which Fromm was already engaged, as a Marxist sociologist and practicing psychoanalyst: synthesizing Marxism and psychoanalysis. The lengthiest contribution Fromm made to this project during his time working for the Institute was his seminal 1930s study of the "authoritarian character" in Weimar Germany.

Based on a series of lengthy "interpretive questionnaires," Fromm found that roughly 10% of 1930s Germans were "authoritarian," roughly 15% were "democratic"/humanistic, and 75% were between the two extremes on the spectrum.[13] The authoritarians, Fromm predicted, would support the Nazis, while the humanists would stand up to and oppose the Nazis. On the face of it, these odds looked good: the authoritarians were clearly outnumbered by the democratic humanists, and the people in the middle said they were politically opposed to fascism. However, Fromm found that the humanistic 15% might prove unable to defeat the authoritarian 10%, if the 75% in the middle were *psychologically unprepared to resist the authoritarians* and decided to submit and thereby cooperate with them. Concluding that the large middle majority did not have the will to resist the Nazis, Fromm realized that the results of the study boded ill. The Institute soon went into exile from Nazi Germany, moving to New York.

Participants in Fromm's study answered numerous open-ended questions in their own words, and Fromm paid close attention to how answers were formulated. He found, for example, when asked about their heroes, some listed

Karl Marx and V.I. Lenin among their heroes, unsurprisingly for Germany at that time. However, *how* the participants listed Marx mattered a lot. While one cited as heroes, "Marx, Lenin, Caesar, and Napoleon," another listed, "Marx, Lenin, Einstein, and Beethoven." The first list, focusing on power and military might, Fromm classified as an authoritarian list, while the latter list implied admiration for "benefactors of humanity" (contributors to thought, politics, science, the arts, etc.).[14] Fromm found that most who scored high on the authoritarianism scale were politically on the right, but he also identified left-wing authoritarians (such as the individual who admired both Marx and Napoleon). Fromm understood that authoritarianism could not be measured solely by professed beliefs or political affiliation. Some authoritarians, he believed, are "rebels" who defy authority but are merely resentful of the powerful because they desire power for themselves and desire the admiration of the powerful.

In addition to the authoritarian rebel, some authoritarians may be "fanatics," appearing very radical due to their intense passion and single-minded devotion to a cause, but who are cold and mechanical, viewing people as instruments for their aims rather than dignified ends in themselves. Rebels and fanatics can appear anti-authoritarian, but each is highly authoritarian (the rebel because the rebel desires power for themselves; the fanatic because the fanatic is submissive to the authoritarian power of their "great cause").[15]

Fromm's study of authoritarianism in Germany, later published as *The Working Class in Weimar Germany*, formed a significant basis for the Frankfurt School's 1940s studies of U.S. antisemitism, studies leading to Theodor Adorno, et al.'s *The Authoritarian Personality* (1950) and Leo Lowenthal and Norbert Guterman's study of the antisemitic "agitator" (propagandist), *Prophets of Deceit: A Study of the Techniques of the American Agitator* (1949). In *The Authoritarian Personality*, Adorno concluded that the social "function" of antisemitism was "as a device for effortless 'orientation' in a cold, alienated, and largely ununderstandable world"[16]—i.e., a pathological way of coping with capitalist alienation. Lowenthal and Guterman similarly wrote at length about the fascist agitator's appeal to the audience's sense of "malaise" and "homelessness." Adorno and Lowenthal agreed with a core claim of Fromm's analysis of fascism—that people sought solace in its authoritarian worldview because they were fleeing a void of meaning.

Although not cited by Adorno or Lowenthal in *The Authoritarian Personality* and *Prophets of Deceit*, Fromm's best-selling *Escape from Freedom* had earlier addressed the same theme of fascism as an adaptation to feelings of malaise and homelessness or to a world apparently lacking in meaning. Expanding on his study of Weimar Germany, Fromm published *Escape from Freedom* in 1941, arguing that fascism emerges partly from a desire to flee the burdens of a limited kind of freedom offered by capitalism. Fromm wrote, "The structure of modern society affects man in two ways simultaneously: he becomes more independent, self-reliant, and critical, and he becomes more isolated, alone, and afraid."[17]

The experience of freedom created by the modern world is incomplete, leaving the individual with many new "negative freedoms" not previously possible under medieval feudalism—e.g., the *freedom from* the state's encroachment on freedom of speech or religion—but without a sense of "positive freedom," a sense of what freedom can be *for*. Humanity, according to Fromm, has gained freedom of religion but "lost to a great extent the inner capacity to have faith in anything which is not provable by the methods of the natural sciences" and has gained freedom of speech but "has not acquired the ability to think originally," submitting instead to the "anonymous authorities" of "public opinion and 'common sense.'"[18]

In *Escape from Freedom*, Fromm identified three interrelated "mechanisms of escape" from freedom, all of which I believe can be seen in contemporary as well as past fascist movements: sadomasochism (as the desire to control and hurt others and to be controlled and hurt), destructiveness, and conformity. These three mechanisms work together, playing off one another, and Fromm would probably hold that an individual with strong tendencies toward a particular mechanism is likely to have characteristics belonging to the other two as well. "Destructiveness," the totalizing or nihilistic violence displayed by some fascists (such as the accelerationists addressed in the next chapter), underlies all fascist ideology and seems like the fullest expression and logical outcome of fascism. According to Fromm, "destructiveness" arises from feelings of powerlessness, fear ("feeling...threatened by the world outside"), and the stifling of life opportunities or potential.[19]

Today we find among youth on the far-right such phenomena as "black pilling," convincing oneself and others the merits of despair, and accompanying images of violence and "nihilist memes," alongside a suicidal and murderous desire to "go out" with some kind of meaning (e.g., dying while perpetrating a mass shooting). In "incel" ("involuntary celibate") spaces, and in white nationalist spaces, there is talk of the choice between "cope" and "rope"—survival in a state of willful blindness to reality and suicidality. These themes express feelings of powerlessness and lost opportunity mingled with destructiveness. Although fascists are wrong in their assessment of the causes of their malaise and alienation, and are responsible for the harm they do, these feelings nonetheless are real.

In this context, I think often of one incident in particular that became a meme among fascists and the far-right. In summer 2018, a disturbed young man stole a plane from the SeaTac airport and flew it successfully for some time, performing a "barrel roll," before finally crashing into the ocean and dying. Futilely trying to humor him and help him land safely, air traffic controllers in communication with him from the ground suggested he might be able to get a job as a pilot if he managed to land the plane. "Yeah, right, I'm a white guy," he answered, believing his race was what disqualified him from such easy success. The man, who became popularly remembered as "Sky King," became the subject of mournful memes. He was surely wrong that his whiteness prevented him from achieving his dreams—if anything, it helped him—and one would rightly wonder whether, for example, a Muslim Middle Eastern man stealing a plane would have been counseled about future career options or just shot down. But the fantasy of a declining modern world that has no role for a white man who nevertheless reaches higher, checks the boxes to achieve fascination and meme-ification. These tendencies often take more outwardly violent forms. Fascist nihilistic destructiveness often desires to "take others down with it," and black-pilling quickly ends in the "gamification" of mass killing, with mass shooters' kill counts referred to in online spaces as "scores."

According to Erich Fromm, the logic of fascist destructiveness receives support from sadomasochistic authoritarianism, which views humans as classifiable according to two static categories: the good, strong winners and the bad, weak losers.[20] This need not be viewed in a strictly sexual sense—I do not think people's sexual fantasies or kinks map neatly onto their individual social character, and Fromm himself was careful on this, though perhaps less so than most critical social theorists would be today. Rather than sadomasochism being expressed in sexual acts, the sadomasochist believes in two kinds of people, with each deserving their status. (This claim is echoed in a speech by "alt-right" fascist Richard Spencer arguing for a return to a Nietzschean "master morality," according to which, "We are strong. We rule. We are good. They, the others, are weak. They are bad."[21]) Conformity further assists the fascist's flight from freedom, as the fascist no longer needs to have his own ideas or act with awareness as an independent moral agent.

"Destructiveness," for Fromm, does not cover all acts of aggression; in his later work *The Anatomy of Human Destructiveness*, Fromm carefully distinguished between "benign aggression" and "malignant aggression."[22] Action in self-defense or fierce competition in a game, for example, is not evidence of a destructive personality (or malignant aggression). By contrast, the destructive personality has a more totalizing destructive aim. The destructive personality takes vengeance on the world for its own "unlived life."[23] In other words, the destructive personality is not one that is merely defending itself, though it may claim to be doing so (defending against "white genocide" or other conspiracy theories about the alleged persecution of white people by people of color or Jews). Rather, it desires a totalizing annihilation.

Destructiveness has its roots in a range of social conditions, according to Fromm. While destructiveness can arise from repression of sexual desire, as capitalism has transformed from exulting restraint to license, other causes of destructiveness have become more prominent—people still have "unlived lives" to avenge due to other factors. Among these factors is, no doubt, not only economic poverty but also forms of alienation and loneliness, which can impact those who are not suffering from crushing poverty but which can also have economic and political bases.[24] (Hannah Arendt also writes of loneliness as caused by and reinforced by totalitarian societies,[25] and others have written on the loss of social relations in modern society, resulting in a "lonely crowd," in sociologist David Riesman's terms.) Today this loneliness and isolation surely contributes to many people's reliance on the internet for social connection; fascists use the internet to form recruits into identification with a new "mythic community."[26] The increase in recruitment into the far-right via the internet is inherently connected to loneliness, as well as increasing it. Although the internet can be a source of positive connection for many people, going down far-right "rabbit holes" can increase paranoia and lead to an inability to share and relate with people with more mainstream views. It can lead the individual to further isolate themselves from their prior social connections and get even more committed to far-right or fascist politics.

As a humanistic psychoanalyst, profoundly influenced by Freud but critical of Freud's theory of the death drive, Fromm did not believe that sadism or destructiveness was "natural." Instead, Fromm believed that sadism and destructiveness were responses to social conditions and individual situations.

According to Fromm, human nature is fundamentally good and is not infinitely malleable, but human beings can take on particular "character structures" that become dominant in particular historical and cultural contexts. Although societies value and encourage particular traits of character, individuals do still have a degree of choice within the limits their context and their human nature provide. Fromm refers to this element of choice as "alternativism": the individual is confronted with certain crucial life choices (alternatives) that will shape the individual's character going forward. Part of the role of the activist (or "prophet"), according to Fromm, is to help societies become more aware of their choices of alternatives (e.g., "life or death," in the words of the Book of Deuteronomy; "socialism or barbarism," in the words of Rosa Luxemburg; or "capitalism or survival," to paraphrase the title of Naomi Klein's book on the climate crisis). Fromm believed that individuals had to make a choice to claim their freedom and work toward greater freedom (personally and socio-politically) or to flee from it by means of mechanisms such as destructiveness.

Simone Weil in Dialogue with Fromm on Destructiveness

Like Fromm, philosopher, spiritual writer, and social activist Simone Weil engaged in a study of the "destructive" character structure of some fascists. Also, like Fromm, Weil came from a left-wing Jewish background. (While

Fromm was raised as a religiously practicing Orthodox Jew in Germany, Weil, in France, was raised by secular Jewish anarchists.) Weil's own social action included brave experiments in solidarity and suffering ("affliction"), including working as a factory worker and writing about factory conditions, before later joining the resistance to Franco's fascism in the Spanish civil war. Following an unexpected religious experience in a Portuguese fishing village, Weil's writing took a Christian turn—she identified Christianity as, countering Nietzsche, "pre-eminently the religion of slaves...Slaves cannot help belonging to it, and I among others"—and she sought to synthesize her religious experience with her commitments to worker solidarity and social action.[27]

Although religious mystics like Weil have long sought transcendence through an encounter with God as somehow "absent" and have experienced some kind of spiritual void (the "dark night of the soul"), the question of "the void" emerged for Weil in the way that it did because of her social, economic, and political contexts. Simone Weil's work, as well as Fromm's, was in many ways a response to a crisis of capitalism and the void of meaning opened or heightened by that crisis.

Following World War I, Europeans and Americans were recuperating from a situation of acute emotional, physical, and social trauma and loss of life, when they were also hit with an economic crash. Just following the point at which hopes were high for international workers' revolutions against capitalism, millions of working-class soldiers had died fighting each other in the trenches, energized by nationalism, in a senseless war for capitalist gain and racist, colonial expansion. It was a crisis that touched the "whole person" for the left-wing intellectuals who sought to understand it—it was a spiritual crisis as well as a political one. There was a sense in some political, philosophical, religious, and artistic circles that something may have gone wrong with time itself, that history had somehow stalled, or that reality had somehow "ruptured," since the Enlightenment ideal of progress that had sustained past hopes seemed to have gone so terribly awry and since the promise of some Marxist rhetoric about the coming revolution had fallen short. The "lost generation" of the 1920s hungered for meanings and answers, and there was sometimes a sense that something transcendent (whether divine or human) might be lurking beyond the horizon, preparing to enter and save a humanity gone tragically wrong. This expectation for outside help, of course, had devastating consequences, especially where it took the form of fascist dependence on a leader as rescuer. Keenly aware of this flight into submission but touched by her own mystical encounter with the transcendent, Simone Weil sought frantically to turn the tide, hoping to help the workers distinguish authentic belief from the clinging to idols, and she was convinced, as we shall see, that entering into that encounter with the transcendent required a self-emptying or "de-creation" achieved not only partly through a spiritual asceticism but also through a relinquishment of wealth and a commitment of solidarity to suffering with and for the oppressed.

Like Fromm, Weil identified destructiveness as one of various possible "compensations" (similar to Fromm's "escapes from freedom"). Through compensations, the individual replaces a frightening encounter with reality by a "safer" encounter with deadened ideas or "idols." We might add (and Weil would likely agree) that capitalist modernity increases the temptation to rely on compensations. I would explain that dilemma like this: societies do not come with obvious narratives of meaning attached, and in complex modern societies, there are many more narratives available for selection, to be freely chosen and publicly lived out. Contrary to fascists' claims, "diversity" or "multiculturalism" does not *cause* voids of meaning. Rather, capitalist globalization confronts individuals with a void that in some ways always exists and intensifies its power. Capitalism increases people's sense of anonymity in a world of consumers and interchangeable workers. It increases anomie (that "normlessness" that early sociologist Emile Durkheim cited as a contributing factor to suicide). Capitalism can increase the sense that one is not only no one but also "nowhere" while lacking a sense of belonging that could be larger in scope (such as might be provided by a sense of international, humanistic belonging or cosmopolitanism). Nationalism as a reaction against multiculturalism is an attempt to retreat and hide from the reality of the void, to live in denial, and to replace complexity with idols. It also falsely attempts to solve questions of meaning through "incestuous ties"[28] to place.[29] Fromm writes that nationalism is idolatrous and akin to "incest," and "'Patriotism' is its cult [of worship]...Just as love for one individual which excludes the love for others is not love, love for one's country which is not part of one's love for humanity is not love, but idolatrous worship."[30]

By fracturing social bonds but giving scope for choice, late capitalist modernity creates greater pressure to select and then cling to some sense of identity, even as capitalism also claims to transcend identities, crafting a homogenous world of work and consumption controlled by an ever-shrinking set of corporations. As social relationships are fractured by competition and commodification of life, and work is characterized by a sense of alienation and powerlessness, identity may be sought as a source of stability; in order for it to have staying power, this sense of identity must be "reified"—must be made to seem *natural* despite being artificial.

However, the lack of pre-assigned meaning that makes this quest for identity possible is also, to some extent, endemic to the human condition, as Weil and Fromm understood, even though it is certainly *exacerbated* by capitalism. Reality always exceeds any explanations offered for it. Idols provide temporary relief from the void of meaning that rests at the heart of reality and at the heart of each human being's struggle to make sense of the world. The void should not be bypassed, Weil argues, but is the point at which the divine reveals itself and at which the sacredness of each human being can be known. Both Fromm and Weil see destructiveness as resulting from a type of "idolatry" that serves as a means to flee this void and to avoid the suffering involved in an encounter with it.

Simone Weil, like Erich Fromm, saw destructiveness as a reaction against suffering. Weil wrote that "whoever suffers tries to communicate his suffering (either by ill-treating someone or calling forth their pity) in order to reduce" his suffering.[31] According to Weil, when we try to expel our suffering through inflicting suffering on another, we do so because we know that it unfortunately *works*, at least in the short run; we do feel a sense of relief.[32] The continual downward distribution of suffering that results "is a factor making for social stability,"[33] maintaining order and comfort in positions of power in society, and with nearly everyone able to displace suffering onto someone lower down in the social hierarchy. (Fascism, of course, operates this way, making constant use of bullying and trolling in the meantime, when not able to achieve its genocidal ambitions.) When one is unable to command sympathy from others or feels unable to sufficiently expel one's suffering onto victims through small, subtle acts of sadism, Weil suggests, a nihilistic type of violence emerges. Then, according to Weil, "we attack *what the universe itself represents for us*. Then every good or beautiful thing is like an insult."[34] As we will see later (in Chapter 2), the fascist skullmask network, a more militant wing of today's fascist movements, believes that change can come only through mass chaos and destruction, such as taking down power grids and sabotaging nuclear power plants. It is not just an "enemy" that must be destroyed to make room for something new but the entire social order on this view. This is not really a new development in fascist strategy or ideology— rather, it expresses in clear terms the destructiveness inherent in fascism, as an attack on "the universe itself."

Destructiveness, according to Weil, is a way of "compensating" for the void. She identifies other possible compensations, including "mindless pleasure" and a shallow "hope, either for oneself or for one's children, of occupying a different place in society."[35] (It is worth noting that both these compensations become less widely accessible in periods of economic decline. Critiquing the shallowness of these compensations, in fact, is part of the argument that fascism makes for itself, presenting itself as "deeper," more ancient and mythical, etc.) "Revolution" can also be a compensation, Weil writes, which as a way of filling the void "is ambition transposed to the collective level."[36] Although some might read such a critique of "revolution" as an indication of a conservatism in Weil, one can also read it as a critique of revolution as "compensation," a critique of revolution as *idol*. The ideal of "revolution" as compensation or idol can be seen in the way that many young fascists see themselves as mythic heroes, in an enduring battle of the forces of good against evil, and fantasize about dying in battle.

Here another parallel between Weil and Fromm becomes clear. The Marxist Fromm echoes Weil's critique of revolution as compensation or idol, in his essay on the "Revolutionary Character," where he contrasts the true revolutionary with the fanatic. The fanatic is "exceedingly narcissistic," he writes, and "extremely unrelated, as any psychotic person is, to the world outside." He writes:

> The fanatic…has chosen a cause, whatever it may be—political, religious, or any other—and he has deified this cause. He has made this cause an idol. In this manner, by complete submission to his idol, he receives a passionate sense of life, a meaning of life; for in his submission he identifies himself with the idol, which he has inflated and made into an absolute.
>
> If we want to choose a symbol for the fanatic, it would be *burning ice*. He is a person who is passionate and extremely cold at the same time. He is utterly unrelated to the world, and yet filled with burning passion, the passion of participation and submission to the Absolute.[37]

The fanatic's narcissism is idolatry; "idolatry" in Fromm's sense of the term is not tied to specific religious practices or beliefs but is a technical term akin to the Marxist term "reification," referring to humans' submission to the authority of mere things and concepts, products of humans' own creative action.[38] Through idolatry, the self is deadened, becoming lifeless like the products of its labor, "worshipping" its own product by submitting to an unjust economic system that is itself merely a creation of human activity.[39] Idolatry for Fromm includes nationalism, racism, and "priestly"[40] (blindly bureaucratic, institutional) loyalties.

For our purposes here, we note that idols include objects of devotion created by human beings, including their (socially constructed, therefore artificial) nation or race. Clearing away idols (ceasing one's obsessive devotion to concepts such as nation or race) is not about removing symbols of transcendence nor about preventing the activity of relating to objects or symbols as manifestations of divine or transcendent realities. Rather, the struggle against idolatry in the Frommian and Weilian sense is a process of *exposing illusions so that the truth can be known*. Revolutionary struggle against idols leads us "beyond the chains of illusion."

Fromm also links idolatry to ideology. Ideology in the traditional (Marxist) sense of the term implies a false belief system ("false consciousness") and is not a neutral term applying to any worldview. Ideology depends upon the "idolatry of words," having the power to detach words from their affective (emotional) meaning and leading individuals to repeat doctrinal platitudes that lack actual bearing on one's life praxis. For example, in the 1950s, Fromm notes that a majority of Americans, if asked whether "all men are created equal," would agree.[41] (After all, this is a central professed belief for many, found in the Declaration of Independence as well as religious traditions.) However, this slogan remained just that—a mere slogan or idol, not a "living idea" that could have bearing, for example, on perhaps the most crucial question of the 1950s context, namely segregation and Jim Crow. Although all might agree that "all men are created equal," the idea behind the words did not have any emotional or practical bearing on everyone. Weil engaged in a similar critique of ideology. In her essay "The Power of Words," Weil wrote that the worst and bloodiest conflicts center around words whose meanings are elusive or non-existent.[42] Nationalism, in particular, she argued, served to fuel conflicts since the concept of the nation is fundamentally empty, finding its only real expression in war.[43] "It is the very concept of the nation that needs to be suppressed—or rather, the manner in which the word is used," she wrote. "For the word national and the expressions of which it forms [a] part are empty of all meaning; their only content is millions of corpses, and orphans, and disabled men, and tears and despair."[44]

To return to the compensations for the void: clearing away "idols" (like nationalism and white supremacy) is a revelation of reality, a reality initially experienced—as Medieval mystics suggested, and Fromm and Weil apply to their context—as empty, dark, and "void." On Weil's account, personal identity cannot be uncovered through artificially trying to recreate the past nor through veneration of the nation-state, because one's true identity is uncovered only through self-emptying, or what Weil calls "decreation" (de-creation).

Importantly, Weil distinguishes between decreation and destruction.[45] Decreation is not violence turned inward against the self but a creative principle that stands in relationship with non-being. According to Weil's philosophical theology, even God's act of creation involved decreation, withdrawing in part from creation to create so that God (as Being) could create something other, a composite of being and non-being.[46] Human beings can participate with God in creating by decreating themselves, withdrawing from their ego and their identification with self-descriptions.[47]

On the face of it, decreation sounds a bit like a weakening of the ego that only the powerful and arrogant should undertake, while people who are oppressed and suffering should strengthen it; I am open to this critique of Weil, and any advice concerning decreation given to people disengaging from hate should also be done with care: decreation cannot be taken to mean self-harm, degradation, ego-stripping, or brainwashing (all things they may have already experienced in the cultish milieus that foster hate). But the key component of decreation—freeing the self from constraining descriptions through consciously sacrificing the comfort they provide—has emancipatory potential for those engaged in hate movements or oppressive violence.

What holds us back from decreation, according to Weil, is our knowledge that after clearing away idols, reality will be experienced as empty, dark, and "void." We know about the void in advance of fully facing it, because we periodically experience the terror of the void when we momentarily release our grip on our idols or glance away from them momentarily before turning back to them in fright. Periodic loss of one idol may lead us to quickly replace it with a new one. Consider the well-known phenomenon of recovering addicts converting to new religions or rapidly becoming more religious; no doubt some of these conversions reflect sincere confrontations with the void—some peered into the void without the help of their past crutches, and something appeared there to them; they had some kind of experience of the transcendent—while others may, in fact, have rushed into the arms of faith in pursuit of a new compensation for the void. The existential freedom of choice combined with apparent meaninglessness that one experiences with the loss of idols can be terrifying, leading one to seek out new authorities (divine, human, or otherwise) to which one can submit. (Notice that not all self-descriptions are idols requiring decreation. It is the *relationship* between the individual and her beliefs that determines whether those beliefs are idolatrous or the result of a sincere confrontation with reality.)

According to Weil, we instead need to hold the void open to *let the void speak*. Filling up the void with whatever we can quickly find only succeeds in drowning out the voice of the "afflicted" (the suffering or oppressed ones) and the voice of God or truth. Filling the silence with the noise of slogans and certainties, we sacrifice our freedom for a tyranny of false ideas.

Although Fromm became an atheist in his late 20s and moved away from the religious practice of his upbringing, he speaks in a similarly mystical way about what Weil calls the void. A number of influences are at play, including Fromm's continued appreciation for the tradition of Jewish negative theology, especially as found in Moses Maimonides in the Middle Ages and the adoption of Maimonides' work by Jewish neo-Kantian socialist philosopher Hermann Cohen[48] in the early twentieth century, who saw Maimonides' negative theology as a humanism.[49] In Fromm's view of this wider Jewish theological and political tradition, the refusal to describe God is a refusal to limit God, and a similar commitment can be applied to human potential and the aims of social struggle. Despite not being a religious believer, Fromm never lost a passion for the power of the mystical negative way.

Fromm's commitment to rejecting idols as means of filling the void allowed him to build alliances and dialogue across religious and cultural traditions. He found elements of the same commitment in Zen Buddhism, as well as in the philosophies of Karl Marx and Meister Eckhart. Fromm's extensive correspondence with Trappist monk, writer, and Catholic peace activist Thomas Merton may also have influenced Fromm's interest in the *via negativa*, and it may have been Fromm who first introduced the work of Simone Weil to Thomas Merton.[50] The same could be said of his engagement with emancipatory pedagogical theorists like Ivan Illich and Paulo Freire, who challenged authoritarian educational models. Refusal to fill the void can be the basis of what Fromm calls "the common struggle against idolatry": the formation of new communities, identities, and social movements around the shared project of embracing "living ideas" and unfolding traditions, not dead concepts and idols. This common struggle unites humanists of all stripes in defense of reason and compassion. Fromm writes:

> Those who participate [in the common struggle against idolatry] must be able to talk from their heart and to the heart. They must not fear to displease anybody, and must consider that reducing hate and arrogance within themselves must be one of their daily efforts.[51]

Simone Weil's mysticism resembles that of Saint John of the Cross, Saint Theresa of Avila, or Meister Eckhart, and activists can be excused for thinking such a tradition would have little to say to the problem of fascism today. Yet I feel compelled to agree with Weil that fascism is in some sense a spiritual problem, by which I mean precisely *not* that it is a problem of dogma but that it is a problem of the intellectual and emotional relationship of the individual to their ideas, a problem with which Medieval mysticism was deeply concerned. It follows from this that the fascist does not *primarily* need to be convinced of the truth of a different set of facts—e.g., to be sat down and convinced that the Holocaust really did happen, IQ does not work such and such a way, and so forth—but rather, the fascist needs a new relationship to truth altogether.

Regardless of one's religious beliefs, we can achieve a new perspective on how to fight fascism by considering what it would mean to ground our praxis and alliances on refusal to fill the void, or on what Fromm called "the common struggle against idolatry." This also gives us a new perspective on who our most natural allies are in the fight against fascism. If Weil and Fromm are correct in their distinction between idolatry and genuine belief, then a Christian like Weil may have more in common with an atheist like Fromm than either of them have in common with those who adopt those beliefs to defend nationalistic hate. Both the Weilian mystic and the Frommian atheist refuse to fill the void. In the next section, I look at how the triad of *void, idol*, and *destructiveness* plays out in recent and contemporary fascist movements in the United States.

The Void in Recent and Contemporary U.S. Fascist Movements

Today's resurgent fascism is a failure to face and encounter the void, stuffing the void instead with hateful mythologies, slogans, pseudo-philosophies and pseudo-science, and eventually violence. The refusal to "sit with" the void, to attend and wait for reality to present itself, leads to stuffing the void with phony identities that are always at risk of coming apart. To prevent anyone from pulling away the mask and revealing a self that is still void—rather than "very deep," as alt-right agitator of the early Trump era, Richard Spencer, insists white identity is—the ideologists of hate employ intimidation and cruelty. "Denialism"[52] is at the heart of the fascist enterprise, and nothing—not even the bullying "humor" for which the "alt-right" has become so widely known—can hide the reality of fascists' superficiality, banality, and evil.

Fascist movements clearly have multiple causes that can be analyzed through multiple lenses and frameworks. In understanding the individual's choice to participate (excluding those who are coerced, such as young children of white supremacists), individuals who engage in hate and violence are and should be held morally responsible, as well as legally responsible when applicable. Structural forces or psychological influences are not morally exculpatory. Expelling one's suffering onto a scapegoated Other in order to avoid the reality of the void is a decision—a decision that one can potentially forgo. However, the rage, entitlement, or frantic clinging to "identity" found among fascists are not explainable simply by an individual propensity to evil. Racism and other forms of hate made normal in mainstream society can increase people's propensity to adopt a fascist worldview, while other psychological and social causes also exist.

Accounts by current and former fascists demonstrate that the appeal of the movement lies partly in its proffering a solution to a search for belonging, meaning, and an outlet for repressed rage. This reflects Fromm's and Weil's work on fascism as an attempt to "escape from freedom" or to use idols to flee voids of meaning, as well as the theme of "destructiveness" in both thinkers. One can also see the ways in which destructiveness is used by fascists' past and present to defend idols and cover the self's emptiness from the awareness of others and oneself.

Asked by One People's Project's Daryle Lamont Jenkins what he was getting out of this, a member of white nationalist group Identity Evropa answered without hesitating: "Purpose, identity, community—what everybody wants."[53] In fact, both Identity Evropa (which later renamed as American Identity Movement and dissolved in 2020) and the National Policy Institute (a propaganda organ of one of the main alt-right leaders of the early Trump era, Richard Spencer) expressed this theme in their online promotional videos and literature. For example, a National Policy Institute video, "Who are We?" begins with Richard Spencer asking, "Who are you? I'm not talking about your name or your occupation. I'm talking about something bigger, something deeper…Today, we seem to have no idea who we are. We are rootless."[54] National identity cannot be based on "abstractions and buzzwords" like democracy, freedom, tolerance, and multiculturalism, he continues.[55] "Man doesn't live and die for freedom. Man lives and dies for a homeland."[56] One is reminded of Lowenthal's assertion that the agitator "drives [listeners] into a *moral void* in which their inner voice of conscience is replaced by an externalized conscience: the agitator himself. He becomes the indispensable guide in a confused world."[57] Richard Spencer not only promises to fill a void, but he also begins by trying to make this sense of void acute before offering himself as a guide through the darkness. "Become who you are" reads a white nationalist group's poster.[58] The phrase presents the lost past identity as a future self—a reunion of self with identity. But who is the "you" who is invited to "become"? The audience must first be stripped of its true sense of self—confused, lost in the void—and surrender its sense of self to the movement, in order to "become" and again have an identity.

In a summer 2017 speech at a fascist "Free Speech Rally," Nathan Damigo, founder of now-defunct white nationalist group Identity Evropa, polemicized, "Fuck your freedom! Give me responsibility!"[59] to cheers from the small crowd. Although he clarified concerning his support for freedom of speech (a talking point of the rally), Damigo stressed a fidelity to past and future white generations as a substitute for freedom. Although "responsibility" might on the surface sound like what the person escaping from freedom seeks to avoid, it is important to note that when counter-posed with freedom in this way, responsibility implies submission. Submission to a cause, group, or leader can be the sort of "responsibility" that stands opposed to freedom; like Erich Fromm's "fanatic," Damigo speaks as an authoritarian, escaping from freedom by submitting to the power of his "great cause." "We aren't fighting for freedom...we aren't fighting for the Constitution," Spencer offers in another speech. "We are fighting for meaning in our lives."[60]

In an excellent *Nation* article, "The Racist Right Looks Left," Donna Minkovitz writes:

[Mike Peinovich, known as "Mike Enoch" and co-host of the antisemitic alt-right *The Daily Shoah* podcast] talked about how hard it is to live in this culture, where "everything" runs the risk of getting "corporatized and capitalized." The Upper East Sider said, sounding haunted, "Everything is empty and fake...One of the great struggles that everyone has in this corporate neoliberal world is for meaning in their life. Our struggle provides that for us. Everything else is empty...but our movement."[61]

Everything else is empty. This is a frequent theme. The adoption of far-right, fascist, or white nationalist politics is introduced as meaning-giving to the depressed individual for whom all else is meaningless. The ideology contains a critique of capitalism cribbed partly from the left but offers as a solution the annihilation of freedom, of self, and of the search for truth in the conventional sense (not fascism's conception of truth as the violent external confirming of internal feelings evoked by the ideology).

Despite the frequent use of "facts" in the rhetoric of today's fascists, who fetishize debunked "race science" studies and may claim their opponents care more about feelings than truth, fascists are, in fact, driven not by an objective use of scientific reason, so much as by a coldly passionate ("fanatical") defense of their idols. They must constantly be assuring themselves that "white identity is very deep" and complex (Richard Spencer) and shoring up feelings of devotion to their ideological idols. Otherwise, their "frame of orientation" (in Fromm's terminology), which has become their new sense of personal identity, is at constant risk of dissolution. The fragility of this new identity is also brought home by remarks by white nationalist leader Patrick Casey (a past leader of white nationalist group Identity Evropa/American Identity Movement), who also uses the term "void," in a May 2018 podcast shared on Identity Evropa's Twitter: Casey's interlocutor asks about the problem of "suicide by alt-right, where people obliterate themselves by adopting the most edgelord tactics and language...to make sure they can never have any social standing." Casey responds, "When you're on the dissident right... it's almost as if there's this void in the middle, or a black hole, and you're dancing around it, and that's just the chaos of the times that we live in."

In listening to Richard Spencer's speeches (which I do not much recommend as a use of one's limited time on this earth), one gets the impression that Spencer's two favorite words are "deep" and "interesting," as though he was constantly trying to convince his listeners and himself that his ideology is not shallow and banal. The white race and white self are "deep," according to Spencer, which one gets the impression he hopes will be believed on faith. The constant defensive professions of fascists about the "depth" and "meaning" of their ideology come off less like enthusiastic expressions of a real experience or even "optics" (marketing) and more like a desperate clinging to the aspiration of finding fulfillment in a largely failing enterprise.

The Void and Former Fascists

Fascists' profession of finding in their ideology an escape from a void of meaning is paralleled at the other end by the words of former members of fascist and far-right movements speaking about their experience of entering as well as departing their past movements. "The void" has become a talking point among some prominent "formers" now engaged in deradicalization projects, describing the process of leaving hate groups and finding new sources of meaning and social connection.[62]

One such former who now does work in hate group disengagement, Christian Picciolini, speaks in his memoir of needing to confront and pass through a "void" on his journey out of hate, comparing facing the void to driving off a cliff:

The French have a saying, *l'appel du vide*, "the call of the void." It describes that tiny voice in your head that even the most rational people might hear, that taunts you to jerk the steering wheel into oncoming traffic, or the feeling when you look over the edge of a steep precipice and become gripped with the fear of falling, but the terrifying impulse to throw yourself off the edge still beckons. In the five years since I had left the [neo-Nazi] movement, I had heard that nagging little voice constantly, always whispering in my ear to find a way to try to kill what I'd helped create, but I was frightened of the consequences…It was time to face the truth. I stepped hard on the gas and drove off that metaphorical cliff. I floored it, content that the demons inside of me were falling to their death. And only then, when I'd allowed that painful, symbolic death to occur—the twisted hunk of my former self burning on the sharp rocks below—only then could I rise from the rubble and begin anew.[63]

The image here, of needing to kill off one sense of self in order to make way for another, resonates with Weil's discussion of decreation. The loss of a fascist identity requires the ability to destroy one's sense of self and the courage and openness to await a new perspective.

Writing after the fact about leaving a hate group in her teenage years, Elisa Hategan said she felt "hollow" and faced an "abyss" as she confronted the task of leaving the group: with a "great chasm" inside, "without any identity…hollow as a bullet," a "shell"[64] with a scrambled confusion inside. As she began to humanize the Heritage Front's victims and reject the group, she writes,

half of me stood on the precipice, political manifesto in one hand, naïve ideals in another. Across the great and dark abyss, a newer-born fragment of my consciousness was shaking, empty-handed, peering stubbornly into the void below in search of a glimmer, an infinitesimal spark of something that she herself didn't know if she could recognize.[65]

A teenager leaving and returning to neo-Nazi groups in Germany said, "Like, I had a choice, right, like go back to my people or be completely alone. That's not a choice."[66] It *is* a choice, though—that's the whole point. While helping people leave hate groups would include some notion of accompaniment through the abyss, the experience of aloneness is inevitable. This young person was not willing to endure that process yet. A deradicalization group staffer said of the teen, "We couldn't hold him. It's like he sees the pit, jumps in, and wonders how he got there."[67]

Katie McHugh, who more recently left white nationalist circles, has cited Saint Augustine's writings as helping her to rethink her ideas. (She has turned over a massive amount of information to the Southern Poverty Law Center and deeply regrets her past involvement in hate.) She told me that she thinks the conservative worldview is mired in "the heresy of Manichaeism, the belief that there are two Gods with dueling creations," a belief that "was channeled into nascent fascism or into upholding the neo-liberal superstructure." On this view, she says:

> Some people are "nice," "good," and thus must have been created by your God—but other people are so unfair and unjust that they must have been created by the rival, Evil God...people who are "mean," "unfair." I believe the conservative mind is deeply Manichaean, especially nowadays. The poor are "ungrateful," "looters" (as my father called me for applying for SNAP and Medicaid), "violent," "uncouth," and so on...When I was in D.C., everyone had fully accepted a Manichaean outlook.

Leaving behind a far-right worldview in which everyone is easily classifiable as friend or foe casts one into a state of confusion, as well as shame in recognizing that one's "enemy" was, in fact, one's victim.

Exiting hate groups means leaving behind one's sense of personal identity before having a substitute, and since members of such groups have sometimes cut themselves off from previous family and friend connections, it can mean leaving behind one's whole social circle and stepping alone into a world perceived as both meaningless and hostile. Unsurprisingly, depression at this stage is common, and the temptation to return to the racist movement can be very strong for some. There can also be a temptation to run quickly to new idols. In fact, one former described his conversion to Christianity as adopting a new idol, saying that he had "exchanged one idol [extremism] for another [Christ]."[68]

Implications of the Void

The ways in which fascism exploits and then distorts the search for meaning remind us on the left that while we must confront fascism, we must also begin to construct alternatives to capitalism and the status quo, including the cultivation of culture, spaces, and dual-power alternatives, to begin to build now the future we seek so that the angry and alienated do not find the far-right to be the only source of meaning or belonging on offer.

The void itself is not the ultimate aim of confrontation with its reality, and individuals need not struggle wholly alone in their confrontation with it. There are alternatives—successful paths through the void. Weil and Fromm suggest that the only way out of the void is *through* it. Both Weil and Fromm distinguish idolatry from a true encounter with transcendence, and distinguish mere fanatics from genuine revolutionaries, who are motivated by love and by their ideals and not by a desire to destroy.

Although, according to Simone Weil, the void is felt as a separation from others and from God, this separation reveals a "something more," a yearning of the human heart that makes what lies beyond perceptible through its absence.[69] The loss of idols is not a loss of truth and meaning but reveals the fundamental need for human meaning and the ways in which that meaning cannot be filled with superficial ideologies. It is the absence of past idols that reveals reality, that allows it to breathe and speak.

Weil's philosophy intentionally offers a psychological and spiritual antidote to fascism, but it is Fromm who offers perhaps the clearer articulation of a broader social movement that can confront the void and ultimately liberate us from it. These two radical thinkers, Weil and Fromm, were students of the many social conditions that give rise to hate. However, they also showed us the nature of the existential or spiritual journey through which we may transcend those conditions both individually and socially. The nature of this journey, involving critical thinking, openness, and questioning, suggests that thinking about "deradicalization" may require more than a therapeutic response or instilling new "narratives" or messages in the individual but rather an educative process as well, including philosophical exploration. A deeper education around issues of racism and other oppressions is needed as well, transcending the often meager, "colorblind" messaging of the counter-extremism industry and digging into deeper questions of justice, including ongoing histories of oppression and resistance.

In the next chapter, I look at how narratives of apocalyptic violence—of destroying and remaking the world—have occupied fascists and the far-right and why and how we must understand the difference between fascist apocalyptic "accelerationism" and leftist revolutionary aspirations. When the logic of fascism leads it to accelerationism (in its hatred of "every good and beautiful thing," to quote Weil's description of destructiveness as compensation), it manifests in action aimed at broad destruction—but this action is no less political, ideological, or planned despite how sweeping its violent aspirations. There I challenge the reader not to see the outward destructiveness and "extremist" appearance of destructiveness as the problem but rather its internal character: its hatred of humanity and human potential and its despair about the possibility of truth or justice.

Notes

1 I use the term "intellectual empathy" here in distinction from Roger Griffin's term "methodological empathy," which is different in meaning. Griffin's "methodological empathy" is based on a rejection of the Marxist analysis of fascism and instead defines fascist ideology by taking fascists' own statements about their beliefs at face value. Notably, that is not what I am doing here, since as I argue in this chapter following the Marxist Critical Theory tradition, fascists often use language for posturing, violence, or aesthetics, and the deeper meaning of their statements is often unconscious (Roger Griffin, *Fascism: An Introduction to Comparative Fascist Studies* [Cambridge: Polity, 2018]).

2 See my chapter, Joan Braune, "A Partial Typology of Empathy for Enemies: Collaborationist to Strategic," in *No Pasarán: Readings on Fascism and Resistance*, ed. Shane Burley. There I delve more deeply into the question of empathy for fascists, outlining some forms of empathy that facilitate fascism or are self-destructive and other forms of empathy for enemies that can still be radical and oppositional, not collaborating with fascists.

3 Joan Braune, "Void and Idol: A Critical Theory Analysis of the Neo-Fascist 'Alt-Right'," *Journal of Hate Studies* 15, no. 11 (2019): 11–37.

4 Christian Picciolini, *Breaking Hate: Confronting the New Culture of Extremism* (New York: Hachette Books, 2020), xxxii.

5 Helen Rose Fuchs Ebaugh, *Becoming an Ex: The Process of Role Exit* (Chicago: University of Chicago Press, 1988), 143–5.

6 Federico Finchelstein, *A Brief History of Fascist Lies* (Oakland: University of California Press, 2020), 24–26.

7 See, for example,

- Michael Kimmel, *Healing from Hate: How Young Men Get Into and Out of Violent Extremism* (Oakland: University of California Press, 2018), 9.
- Christian Picciolini, *Breaking Hate: Confronting the New Culture of Extremism* (New York: Hachette Books, 2020).
- Julian Paffrath and Bernd Simon, "The Significance of the Superordinate: Linking (Dis) Embedded Identity to Non-Normative Ends and Means," *The Journal of Deradicalization* 24 (Fall 2020): 161–90. Paffrath and Simon argue that moving individuals from over-identification with an in-group to "identification with society" is necessary for achieving "order and stability" in society
- Tiana Gaudette and Ryan Scrivens, et al., "Upvoting Extremism: Collective Identity Formation and the Extreme Right on Reddit," *New Media & Society* 23(2020): 1–18.

8 Noted in Kimmel, *Healing from Hate*, 6–7. E.g. Tore Bjorgo, "Dreams and Disillusionment: Engagement in and Disengagement from Militant Extremist Groups," *Crime Law and Social Change* 55 (2011): 277–85.

9 "SAVE Supporting Document: Becoming a Former: Identity, Ideology, and Counterradicalization," *Council on Foreign Relations*, March 22, 2012, https://www.cfr.org/report/save-supporting-document-becoming-former.

10 Cassie Elizabeth Daugherty, "Deradicalization and Disengagement: Exit Programs in Norway and Sweden and Addressing Neo-Nazi Extremism," *Journal for Deradicalization*, 21 (Winter 2019/20).

11 Bjorgo, "Dreams and Disillusionment," 283.

12 Creating profiles of potential extremists can have negative impacts and should generally be avoided. One study, for example, was reported to the public as warning that "extremists" have difficulty with "complex mental tasks"; this media presentation could contribute to ableist fears and profiling and contribute to "attack of the feeble-minded" prejudices that played into American eugenics programs later taken up by the Nazis (e.g., Natalie Grover, "People with Extremist Views Less Able to do Complex Mental Tasks, Research Suggests," *The Guardian*, February 21, 2021, https://www.theguardian.com/science/2021/feb/22/people-with-extremist-views-less-able-to-do-complex-mental-tasks-research-suggests). As Zvi Dav studies, there are many people with autism involved in the far-right, but this should not be attributed to autism itself but rather to ableist and racist social conditions that make people with autism more vulnerable both for recruitment and for victimization by far-right groups. (See Zvi Dav's website https://autismagainstfascism.wordpress.com/ and Dav's podcast interview with Yeah Nah Pasaran. "Zvi

Dav on Autism Against Fascism," December 10, 2020, https://www.3cr.org.au/
yeahnahpasaran/episode-202012101630/zvi-dav-autism-against-fascism.)

13 Erich Fromm, "The Revolutionary Character," *The Dogma of Christ*, ed. Erich
Fromm (New York: Routledge, 2004), 123.

14 Nick Braune, "Erich Fromm's Civics: Sanity, Disobedience, Revolution,"
Progressive Psychoanalysis as a Social Justice Movement, ed. Scott Graybow
(Newcastle: Cambridge Scholars Publishing, 2017), 75.

15 Fromm, "Revolutionary Character," 125–6.

16 Adorno, et al., *The Authoritarian Personality* (New York: Harper, 1950), 608.

17 Fromm, *Escape from Freedom* (New York: Avon Books, 1969), 124.

18 Fromm, *Escape from Freedom*, 125.

19 Fromm, *Escape from Freedom*, 204.

20 Sadomasochism for Fromm is a broad category, not so much about sexual desire
or infliction of pain as about the desire to have power and submit to power.

21 Spencer, "Why Do They Hate Us?" https://www.youtube.com/watch?v=
3SgLSV9Mgfw.

22 Anatomy of Human Destructiveness.

23 Fromm, *Escape from Freedom*, 207.

24 Fromm, *Escape from Freedom*, 207–8.

25 Hannah Arendt, *Origins of Totalitarianism*, 478.

26 12 Rules for What?, *Post-Internet Far Right: Fascism in the Age of the Internet*
(London: Dog Section Press, 2021), 31.

27 Simone Weil, *Waiting for God*, Trans. E. Craufurd (New York: Harper & Row,
1951), 67.

28 Fromm, *The Sane Society*, 57.

29 Cynthia Miller-Idriss, *Hate in the Homeland: The New Global Far Right*.

30 Fromm, *The Sane Society*, 58–9.

31 Simone Weil, "Void and Compensation," *Simone Weil: An Anthology*, ed. Sian
Miles (New York: Grove Press, 1986), 196.

32 Weil, "Void and Compensation," 196.

33 Weil, "Void and Compensation," 197.

34 Weil, "Void and Compensation," 197. [Weil's italics]

35 Simone Weil, "Prerequisite to Dignity of Labour," *Simone Weil: An Anthology*,
ed. Sian Miles (New York: Grove Press, 1986), 246.

36 Weil, "Prerequisite to Dignity of Labour," 246.

37 Fromm, "Revolutionary Character," 126.

38 Erich Fromm, *Marx's Concept of Man* (London: Continuum, 2004), 37–8.

39 Erich Fromm, *On Being Human* (New York: Continuum, 1994), 97.

40 Erich Fromm, "Prophets and Priests," *On Disobedience: Why Freedom Means
Saying "No" to Power* (New York: Harper Perennial, 2010).

41 Fromm, *Man for Himself: An Inquiry into the Psychology of Ethics* (New York:
Henry Holt and Company, 1947), 101.

42 Simone Weil, "Power of Words," *Simone Weil: An Anthology*, ed. Sian Miles
(New York: Grove Press, 1986), 222.

43 Weil, "Power of Words," 225.

44 Weil, "Power of Words," 225.

45 Weil, "Decreation," *Simone Weil Reader*, ed. George Panichas, 350.

46 Weil, "Decreation," 351.

47 Weil, "Decreation," 351.

48 Fromm, *On Being Human*, 143.

49 Hermann Cohen, *The Religion of Reason Out of the Sources of Judaism*, trans.
Simon Kaplan (Atlanta: Scholars Press, 1995), 311.

50 Joan Braune, "Erich Fromm and Thomas Merton: Biophilia, Necrophilia, and Messianism", *Reclaiming the Sane Society: The Life and Scholarship of Erich Fromm in Critical Theory for the 21st Century* (Rotterdam: Sense Publishers, 2014).
51 Fromm, *On Being Human*, 99.
52 Keith Kahn-Harris, *Denial: The Unspeakable Truth* (Mirefoot: Notting Hill Editions, 2018).
53 Jenkins interview with Identity Evropa Members, July 20, 2017, https://www.youtube.com/watch?v=hMCHELIJt14.
54 National Policy Institute, "Who Are We?", July 20, 2017, https://www.youtube.com/watch?v=3rnRPhEwELo.
55 National Policy Institute, "Who Are We?"
56 National Policy Institute, "Who Are We?"
57 Lowenthal, 151 [italics mine].
58 Berry, *Blood and Faith*, 173.
59 "Free Speech Rally – Nathan Damigo," https://www.youtube.com/watch?v=5rcT-k6cFW4.
60 "Free Speech Rally – Richard Spencer," https://www.youtube.com/watch?v=H8q89r2KgCM.
61 Donna Minkowitz, "The Racist Right Looks Left," *The Nation*, December 8, 2017, https://www.thenation.com/article/the-racist-right-looks-left/.
62 E.g., see Jason Wilson on Tony MacAleer, "Life after White Supremacy: The Former Neo-Fascist Now Working to Fight Hate," *The Guardian*, April 4, 2017, https://www.theguardian.com/world/2017/apr/04/life-after-hate-groups-neo-fascism-racism.
63 Christian Picciolini, *White American Youth: My Descent into America's Most Violent Hate Movement—And How I Got Out* (New York: Hachette Books, 2017), 251–2.
64 Elisa Hategan, *Race Traitor: The True Story of Canadian Intelligence's Greatest Cover-Up* (Coppell: Incognito Press, 2014), 177.
65 Hategan, 148.
66 Kimmel, *Healing from Hate*, 62.
67 Kimmel, *Healing from Hate*, 62.
68 Pete Simi, Kathleen Blee, et al. "Addicted to Hate: Identity Residual among Former White Supremacists," *American Sociological Review* 82, no. 6: 1167–1187, 1180.
69 Weil, "Metaxu," *Simone Weil Reader*, ed. Panichas, 363.

Bibliography

12 Rules for What? *Post-Internet Far Right: Fascism in the Age of the Internet.* London: Dog Section Press, 2021.
Adorno, Theodor and Frenkel-Brunswik, E., et al. *The Authoritarian Personality.* New York: Harper, 1950.
Arendt, Hannah. *Origins of Totalitarianism.* Orlando: Harcourt, 1976.
Berry, Damon T. *Blood and Faith: Christianity in American White Nationalism.* Syracuse: Syracuse University Press, 2017.
Bjorgo, Tore. "Dreams and Disillusionment: Engagement in and Disengagement from Militant Extremist Groups. *Crime Law and Social Change* 55 (2011): 277–85.
Braune, Joan. "Erich Fromm and Thomas Merton: Biophilia, Necrophilia, and Messianism", in Seyed Javad Miri, Robert Lake, and Tricia M. Kress, Eds.,

Reclaiming the Sane Society: The Life and Scholarship of Erich Fromm in Critical Theory for the 21st Century (137–146). Rotterdam: Sense Publishers, 2014.

Braune, Joan. "A Partial Typology of Empathy for Enemies: Collaborationist to Strategic," in Shane Burley, Ed., *No Pasarán: Readings on Fascism and Resistance* (388–412). Chico: AK Press and the Institute for Anarchist Studies, 2022.

Braune, Joan. "Void and Idol: A Critical Theory Analysis of the Neo-Fascist 'Alt-Right'." *Journal of Hate Studies* 15, no. 11 (2019): 11–37.

Braune, Nick. "Erich Fromm's Civics: Sanity, Disobedience, Revolution." In Scott Graybow, Ed., *Progressive Psychoanalysis as a Social Justice Movement* (66–81). Newcastle: Cambridge Scholars Publishing, 2017.

Cohen, Hermann. *The Religion of Reason Out of the Sources of Judaism*, trans. Simon Kaplan. Atlanta: Scholars Press, 1995.

Daugherty, Cassie Elizabeth. "Deradicalization and Disengagement: Exit Programs in Norway and Sweden and Addressing Neo-Nazi Extremism." *Journal for Deradicalization*, 21 (Winter 2019/20): 219–60.

Ebaugh, Helen Rose Fuchs. *Becoming an Ex: The Process of Role Exit*. Chicago: University of Chicago Press, 1988.

Finchelstein, Federico. *A Brief History of Fascist Lies*. Oakland: University of California Press, 2020.

"Free Speech Rally – Nathan Damigo." https://www.youtube.com/watch?v=5rcT-k6cFW4.

Fromm, Erich. *Escape from Freedom*. New York: Avon Books, 1969.

Fromm, Erich. *On Being Human*. New York: Continuum, 1994.

Fromm, Erich. *Man for Himself: An Inquiry into the Psychology of Ethics*. New York: Henry Holt and Company, 1947.

Fromm, Erich. *Marx's Concept of Man*. London: Continuum, 2004.

Fromm, Erich. "Prophets and Priests," *On Disobedience: Why Freedom Means Saying "No" to Power*. New York: Harper Perennial, 2010.

Fromm, Erich. "The Revolutionary Character." In Fromm, *The Dogma of Christ* (122–39). New York: Routledge, 2004.

Fromm, Erich. *The Sane Society*. New York: Henry Holt and Company, 1955.

Gaudette, Tiana and Ryan Scrivens, et al. "Upvoting Extremism: Collective Identity Formation and the Extreme Right on Reddit." *New Media & Society* 23, no. 12(2020): 1–18.

Griffin, Roger. *Fascism: An Introduction to Comparative Fascist Studies*. Cambridge: Polity, 2018.

Grover, Natalie. "People with Extremist Views Less Able to do Complex Mental Tasks, Research Suggests." *The Guardian*, February 21, 2021. https://www.theguardian.com/science/2021/feb/22/people-with-extremist-views-less-able-to-do-complex-mental-tasks-research-suggests.

Hategan, Elisa. *Race Traitor: The True Story of Canadian Intelligence's Greatest Cover-Up*. Coppell: Incognito Press, 2014.

Kahn-Harris, Keith. *Denial: The Unspeakable Truth*. Mirefoot: Notting Hill Editions, 2018.

Kimmel, Michael. *Healing from Hate: How Young Men Get Into and Out of Violent Extremism*. Oakland: University of California Press, 2018.

Lowenthal, Leo and Norbert Guterman. *False Prophets: Studies in Authoritarianism, Communication in Society*, Vol. 3. New York: Routledge, 2017.

Miller-Idriss, Cynthia. *Hate in the Homeland: The New Global Far-Right*. Princeton, NJ: Princeton University Press, 2020.

Minkowitz, Donna. "The Racist Right Looks Left." *The Nation*, December 8, 2017. https://www.thenation.com/article/the-racist-right-looks-left/.

National Policy Institute. "Who Are We?" *YouTube*. Link no longer available.

Paffrath, Julian and Bernd Simon. "The Significance of the Superordinate: Linking (Dis) Embedded Identity to Non-Normative Ends and Means." *The Journal of Deradicalization*. 24 (Fall 2020): 161–90.

Picciolini, Christian. *Breaking Hate: Confronting the New Culture of Extremism*. New York: Hachette Books, 2020.

Picciolini, Christian. *White American Youth: My Descent into America's Most Violent Hate Movement—And How I Got Out*. New York: Hachette Books, 2017.

"SAVE Supporting Document: Becoming a Former: Identity, Ideology, and Counterradicalization." *Council on Foreign Relations*, March 22, 2012. https://www.cfr.org/report/save-supporting-document-becoming-former.

Simi, Pete, Kathleen Blee, et al. "Addicted to Hate: Identity Residual among Former White Supremacists." *American Sociological Review* 82, no. 6(2017): 1167–87.

Weil, Simone. *Simone Weil: An Anthology*. Ed. Sian Miles. New York: Grove Press, 1986.

Weil, Simone. *Simone Weil Reader*. Ed. Panichas. New York: David McKay Company, 1977.

Weil, Simone. *Waiting for God*. Trans. E. Craufurd. New York: Harper & Row, 1951.

Wilson, Jason. "Life after White Supremacy: The Former Neo-Fascist Now Working to Fight Hate." *The Guardian*, April 4, 2017. https://www.theguardian.com/world/2017/apr/04/life-after-hate-groups-neo-fascism-racism.

Yeah Nah Pasaran. "Zvi Dav on Autism Against Fascism." December 10, 2020. https://www.3cr.org.au/yeahnahpasaran/episode-202012101630/zvi-dav-autism-against-fascism.

2

DESTRUCTION AND REBIRTH

This chapter explores fascism's mythic, destructive vision. Fascism as a social movement sees itself as the protagonist in the "turning" of a foreordained historical or natural cycle that destroys and rebirths the world. The fascist hero is presented as the mythic destroyer who is foreordained to burn down the world and erect a new one from the ashes. This vision is often "accelerationist," in the sense of trying to speed up this cycle of destruction and rebirth through acting to deliberately worsen present conditions. The term "accelerationism"—and a discussion of its use and misuse by researchers—will figure prominently in this chapter. As we shall see, the term "accelerationism" is in vogue among researchers tracking the far-right. It is often claimed that accelerationism is not "ideological."[1] I demonstrate why this claim can be problematic and discuss what the focus on "accelerationism" gets wrong despite the ways fascism seeks to speed up apocalyptic change.

The network of law enforcement, counterterrorism officials, think tanks, and non-governmental organizations (NGOs) that makes up what some have called the "counter-extremism industry" tends to see danger and a potential indicator of violence in the desire for things to be *dramatically otherwise, very soon*. In fact, it is neither the desire for big change nor the sense of urgency that renders fascism dangerous, but its destructive and eliminationist character, as I will argue. Accelerationism's catastrophic vision must be differentiated from other revolutionary or aggressive impulses with different aims and values. Eliding these distinctions, prevailing narratives of the counter-extremism industry tend to classify "accelerationism" too broadly. This creates confusion about the nature of fascism and opens up space for state targeting of other groups categorized under the same label of "accelerationism."

DOI: 10.4324/9781003031604-3

To distinguish fascist accelerationism from leftist emancipatory, revolutionary movements, I will turn again to the work of Critical Theorist Erich Fromm. As we shall see, Fromm's critique of "catastrophic messianism" was partly a critique of fascist ideology's accelerationist tendencies and continues to hold up today. Fromm's distinction between "catastrophic" and "prophetic" messianisms helps to demonstrate that the revolutionary aspiration for a new humanity and a new time on the part of the left is not reducible to the same impulses as fascist accelerationism.

In what follows, I begin by defining "accelerationism," discussing three meanings of the term, before critiquing the overly broad uses of the term taking hold in the world of counter-extremism and counterterrorism. In particular, I raise concerns about theories that suggest a convergence between different forces, in which the goal of overthrowing the U.S. government supersedes and even undermines ideological differences. I then discuss the difference between "catastrophist" and "prophetic" revolutionary yearnings, showing how the yearning for total transformation takes multiple forms, not all of which converge in theory or practice. Next, I discuss how catastrophist or accelerationist thinking manifests in dehumanizing and eventually eliminationist politics. I conclude the chapter discussing one guiding myth that has long influenced fascist movements: namely, the appropriation of belief in a Hindu cyclical vision of history according to which a present dark age will end through an apocalyptic cataclysm that destroys and remakes the world, restoring past tradition. This sets the stage for the next chapter, on Steve Bannon, in which I address the adoption of this myth by Bannon and the influence on Bannon of the "Traditionalist" fascist authors such as Julius Evola.

Three Meanings of "Accelerationism"

We must distinguish three meanings of the word "accelerationist": (a) a newer network of fascists sometimes called "skullmasks"; (b) a *broader strategic approach* to social change, calling for the violent destruction and disruption of current conditions; and (c) a *philosophical school of thought* with both left-wing and right-wing branches that traces its lineage to British philosopher Nick Land.

First, the term "accelerationist" is often applied to members of an international network of Nazi insurgents sometimes called *skullmasks*, belonging to a set of amorphous and loosely linked organizations with names like Atomwaffen Division, Feuerkrieg Division, and The Base. Nicknamed for their use of skull-image imprinted balaclavas to hide their identities in photographs,[2] the skullmasks embrace violence such as assassinations, mass shootings, bombings, and destruction of infrastructure, as well as the use of disinformation to spread conflict, all carried out by a loose network of armed cells, making it harder for law enforcement to track them. The skullmask network emerged out of the online IronMarch forum, founded in 2011 by an Uzbek man named Alisher Mukhitdinov, who goes by Alexander Slavros.[3] Slavros is only one of a multitude of propagandists who helped to form the network, but since he wrote some of its founding documents, I will rely on his writings later in this chapter to explicate the ideology of the skullmasks.

Second, the term "accelerationism" is also used to refer to a *broader strategic approach* based on the belief that the best or only way to transform society in the direction of one's aims is to first cause chaos, violence, and social collapse. Accelerationists believe that society is so rotten that it can only be changed by being destroyed or profoundly violently disrupted and that history will somehow reset or fix itself following a coming catastrophic event.

Third, there are also some *philosophical schools of thought* termed "accelerationism," which trace their lineage, at least in name, to the work of reactionary British philosopher Nick Land. Land believes that capitalism's technological acceleration and environmental destruction are unstoppable and should be embraced. He also advocates eugenics.[4] Land's philosophy influenced a set of Silicon Valley reactionaries, some of whom were influential on the Trump administration. Leftist accelerationism, by contrast, is animated more by excitement about technology and traces its ideas back to certain statements in Marx, being also influenced by Nietzsche, Deleuze and Guattari, and Mark Fisher. There are also a variety of other accelerationisms, such as gender accelerationism and blaccelerationism (Black accelerationism), which trace their various lineages back to left, right, or both strands of accelerationist thought. Although Land's philosophy has perhaps had some degree of influence on the accelerationist, "skullmask" Nazi movement— some have pointed out that he has made ambiguously favorable comments[5] about the Order of Nine Angles (O9A), a Satanist cult with connections to the skullmask movement—Land is not their leader or founder. I will not be dealing further with Land or the details of accelerationist schools of thought in this chapter, dealing instead with the skullmask network and accelerationism more broadly as a strategy of social change, to explain these violent ways of filling the void and the danger they pose.

Accelerationism and Normalization as Fascist Strategies

Nazi accelerationism can be seen partly as a reaction against *normalization*. Strategies of *normalization* recruit by presenting a friendlier face for fascist politics, seeking to appear as the patriotic, down-home American "boy next door" or "girl next door," rather than presenting an "edgy" or violent image. A fascist pursuing a strategy of normalization would avoid using racial slurs in public or displaying a swastika tattoo, for example, and attempt to appear "clean cut" and "normal." Normalization often uses *entryism* as a tactic. *Entryism* generally refers to those on the political edges (right or left), entering mainstream political parties to shift them further right or left, though I use the term to include attempts to normalize fascist ideology through entering not only political parties but also any mainstream institutions not normally associated with the far-right, such as schools, charities, religious organizations, or labor unions. A strategy of normalization or entryism focuses on "optics," that is, with how one appears personally and how one represents the movement to potential allies.

Accelerationism rejects normalization's concern with optics as naïve and cowardly. The shooter at Pittsburgh's Tree of Life synagogue, who killed 11 people in the 2018 attack, expressed this sentiment, when he wrote before the attack, "Screw your optics. I'm going in." Accelerationists seek to "black pill" those who are pursuing more entryist or normalizing strategies. Although the term "black pill" is often associated with the despair of the misogynistic incel ("involuntary celibate") movement, the term refers more generally to "a bleakly nihilistic mindset in which the world's doom is seen as inevitable."[6] The black pill teaches, as researcher David Neiwert explains, that

> the system is too rotten, the global environment poised for catastrophe, everything is too far gone. So violence becomes not just excusable, but a way of going out, paradoxically, with some kind of meaning, even if it's just the "score" you can roll up in a mass murder, glorified among your fellow trolls at 4chan and Reddit who have, horrifically, "gamified" these killings.[7]

The "gamification" of killings includes calling the death toll of a mass shooting the "score" of the shooter—Nazi accelerationists talk about topping these "scores" and trying to kill more people in each next mass shooting. Particularly perversely, mass shooters are often called "saints" and depicted with religious iconography, to further heroize their acts of slaughter.[8] Even early on, IronMarch was praising killers including Anders Breivik, Timothy McVeigh, Charles Manson, and the Columbine High School shooters. The accelerationist movement mainly attaches new terms and symbols to older ideas. Its strategy is not new but is a repackaging of fascist/white supremacist strategies of "leaderless resistance" or "lone wolf" action.

Another frequently mentioned influence on today's accelerationist fascists is neo-Nazi James Mason's book *Siege*, a series of articles by Mason from the 1980s, published as a book in the early 1990s. Mason traced an evolution from normalizing attempts at respectability to wild destructiveness, "from Commander Rockwell's expressed ideal of the 'American Constitutional Republic' to 'Helter Skelter' [Charles Manson]" and "from 'good citizenship' and conformity to total dropout and total revolution."[9] He described a new reality in which "there are no innocents, no non-combatants":[10]

> We must have acts of revolution, the sooner the better, the more the merrier. But these...can and MUST be carried out by INDIVIDUALS and that removes all requirement for talk, the possibility of "conspiracy," and the danger of a leak! The lone wolf cannot be detected, cannot be prevented, and seldom can be traced.
>
> *(He also suggested training by joining the U.S. military)*

The idea of "leaderless resistance" among neo-Nazis and white supremacists has been around since the 1980s, when there were those pushing for more extreme and violent approaches, like Robert Mathews' The Order (formed in 1983), which conducted numerous bombings, shootings, and robberies. The term itself was coined by Louis Beam of the Aryan Nations, an associate of the Order, at a white supremacist conference in 1992. Beam saw "lone wolf" attacks as part of a strategy of leaderless resistance that would make it more difficult for the government to prevent attacks and that would, Beam hoped, help kick off a race war. The popularity of the novels of white supremacist William Luther Pierce, especially *The Turner Diaries*, also helped to spread enthusiasm in the white power movement for acts of mass destruction, especially bombings. The breakdown of the loose 1980s White Power coalition sought to accelerate through cells and "lone wolves." The term "lone wolf" is often used by journalists and law enforcement to suggest that an individual was not ideologically motivated and was acting alone rather than as a representative of a movement, but this is very different from how this term has been used by those who identify with "lone wolf" violent action.

Here is James Mason in *Siege* again, endorsing the "lone wolf" strategy, but presenting the lone wolf as not just a strategy but also an identity, an individual who has surmounted fear, weakness, and conformity and has achieved transcendence over the rest of humanity:

> You'll become physically and mentally tough. You'll lose any fear. Minus any fanfare or uniform of any kind, even with your commitment a complete secret, you'll stand apart and inspire wonder and respect. You'll in fact be a leader. You'll become resourceful and can make do with nothing. No situation, no opponent will daunt you. You will no longer be "victim" material. You will cease to be part of the herd of sheep but will instead have become a lone wolf. Your inner spirit will feel satisfied because you will know that you are—probably for the first time in your life—fully a part of the quest for actual survival rather than for temporary pleasure and false "security." You'll be rich in your manhood or womanhood. You won't be a slave.

One can see here how white supremacist terror is offered to potential recruits as a promise of superiority and safety and as a response to past suffering or trauma, promising recruits that they will never again be a victim, unsatisfied, forgotten, or helpless.

Although "lone wolf" violence and "skullmask" accelerationist strategies are terrifying by design, fascist strategies of "normalization" can be even more dangerous. While leaderless resistance can be used to carry out mass shootings, take down electrical grids, or poison a town's water supply, normalization facilitates the path toward genocide via institutional policies and mainstream practices. Ultimately, however, the two strategic approaches may be used by the same people, and both approaches involve deception.

Since fascism believes that truth is intuitively known by those destined for power and that it cannot be accessed by those it deems less worthy, fascism does not believe in educating the masses. Beliefs are to be aesthetically performed, and truths are to be created through force rather than rationally uncovered. Normalization conceals fascism's true aims until it can move the window of acceptable public opinion further in its direction. Accelerationism is also dishonest, of course, operating in secrecy and subterfuge and luring recruits first with violent memes, images, videos, and slogans. Recruits are systematically desensitized to violence until mass murder begins to seem like a cynical joke and then to be made reality once individuals have passed the vetting process and trained for violence. IronMarch forum founder Alexander Slavros suggested recruiting to Nazism by using other terms like "conservative revolution" and only later explaining that it was a synonym for Nazism.[11] The tactical dishonesty of accelerationism is also evident in its use of disinformation, like falsely claiming after the Parkland, Florida, school shooting that the shooter belonged to a white nationalist militia.[12] Disinformation is used to disrupt social order and instill fear.

Coalitional Accelerationism: "My Enemies Must Be Friends"[13]

The multiple meanings of accelerationism, as well as some of the limitations of counterterrorism and "radicalization" theory, have created some confusion about accelerationism. Some suggest that accelerationism is a growing coalition of far-right actors who no longer care about ideology or that accelerationism is "anti-ideological." Others even suggest that accelerationism is a growing social phenomenon on both the left and the right.[14] To overcome these confusions, we need to distinguish between shared strategies and shared belief systems.

Those who say that accelerationism undermines ideology do not mean the term "ideology" in the Marxist sense of "false consciousness" (or Fromm's "idolatry of words" discussed in Chapter 1). Rather, they mean the term in its more conventional usage: something like a belief system that includes an assessment (usually including critique) of present society and a belief about a future society to be sought or about a means of attaining that society.

In this sense, the "skullmasks," the Nazi accelerationist network that emerged out of the IronMarch network, certainly have an ideology: simply put, their ideology is fascism. If we are talking about the broader range of people who find an "accelerationist" *strategy* desirable, or who are attempting to worsen conditions to reset history, that is a much broader category of people who do not share a common ideology.

In the article, "Uniting for Total Collapse: The January 6 Boost to Accelerationism," published by the Combating Terrorism Center at West Point, Brian Hughes and Cynthia Miller-Idriss posit a "coalitional accelerationism," changing the nature of the far-right threat of violence in the United States. According to Hughes and Miller-Idriss, a variety of far-right tendencies are amassing around a shared goal of creating social disorder and societal disintegration, or simply the overthrow of governments, such as the U.S. government. They also suggest that this shared motion toward intentionally sowing chaos involves an embrace of destruction *instead of* ideological belief systems. Hughes and Miller-Idriss suggest that the January 6 coup attempt was motivated by "coalitional accelerationism" aimed at overthrowing the government and which they see as "anti-ideological":

> Accelerationism is best understood as an *anti-ideology*, directed toward the destruction of the current ideological order and the political-economic system that expresses and creates that order. But in its anti-ideological thrust, accelerationism makes possible what had once been so difficult: to move the many varieties of extreme far-right tendencies in unison [italics in original].[15]

Let's break this down. First, many organizations and movements across the political spectrum see the U.S. government as an enemy, including various far-right, leftist, and religious fundamentalist groups. Clearly, not all of them were represented at the storming of the U.S. Capitol on January 6, 2021. What the people breaking into the Capitol had in common was their membership in the American far-right, a category that includes but is not limited to self-identified fascists. However, the Capitol rioters came from a variety of different tendencies within the American far-right.

Hughes and Miller-Idriss write of those who stormed the Capitol, calling them accelerationists:

> Accelerationism is not an ideology in itself. Rather, it is an ideological *style* and a strategic method, meant to bring about the failure of the ideologies that prevail in any given system or country at this particular moment in time. In the United States, these systems include representative democracy with a strong federal government, putative equality under the

law, free markets, internationalism, and a highly technological lifestyle in which commercial entertainment and consumption play important roles. Under accelerationism—as a goal and a tactic—individuals with disparate beliefs are united in the goal of hastening the cataclysmic end of economic, political, and social systems so as to more rapidly bring about what is seen as an inevitable end-times collapse and subsequent rebirth into a utopian afterworld [italics authors'].[16]

This framing seems to obscure rather than reveal the events of January 6. While some of those who stormed the Capitol may not have cared about the legitimacy of American presidential elections, some no doubt envisioned themselves as defending what they believed to be the founding spirit or principles of the American system of government from an election they believed to be fraudulent or from a conspiratorial scheme they believed was undermining American society. Far-right militia members who call themselves "patriots" sometimes sincerely conceive of themselves as defending the U.S. Constitution, and on January 6, such people were present alongside people more influenced by white nationalist and Nazi ideologies. Although it is true that people of various ideological tendencies worked together on January 6, this does not mean that accelerationism is anti-ideological (any more than different leftist groups working together would imply that they do not care about the specificities of their own beliefs).

In addition to oversimplifying the January 6 coup attempt, the claim that accelerationism is coalitional due to transcending ideologies has also led to less accurate and less victim-centered or survivor-centered responses to events. In July 2022, a mass shooting in Highland Park, Illinois, was reported as "non-ideological" by National Public Radio and some other media outlets that relied on "experts" on accelerationism for their analysis.[17] This description produced an outcry from some members of the impacted community, including individuals who had experienced the mass shooter's prior bigoted or threatening behavior. The shooter had been influenced by "schizoposting" in internet spaces—a practice promoted by some Nazis of meme-ing about "going schizo" by becoming paranoid and committing mass violence. Since schizoposting was associated with "accelerationism,"[18] the experts' framework implied a need to inform the public that the action lacked "ideological" consistency. This, in fact, proved to be unhelpful. Rather than a nuanced discussion about the ways ideology may or may not have influenced the shooting, half the public heard, "There was nothing political here," while those who felt they belonged to a group targeted by the act may have felt like they were being condescendingly told, "Calm down; this isn't about you."

The tendency to suspect that accelerationists do not have an ideology is also complicated by the association of mass shootings in general with an outbreak of accelerationism. While some mass shooters are clear white supremacists and/or fascists and may have been inspired by the postings of accelerationists on sites like Telegram, many mass shooters lack a clear ideological motive. Attackers with personal grievances may look for an ideological justification and find several, even contradictory, belief systems as justification for their violence.[19] However, the relatively small proportion of people who commit violent mass attacks should not be taken as representative of a rejection of ideological belonging in a wider population of people belonging to militant or accelerationist movements.

"Coalitional accelerationism" claims generate further confusion when they get tangled up in a related but different claim: namely, the claim that specifically the people who are most often called "the accelerationists"—i.e., the "skullmasks," the Nazi movement that had its origins in Slavros's IronMarch forum—themselves lack ideology. This claim is even more puzzling than the first, because, unlike the broader mass of people who showed up to raid the U.S. Capitol, the skullmask accelerationists not only have ideologies individually but also have their own *shared ideology*: namely, fascism. Their version of fascism is not new and draws specifically from the historic Nazi version. The young people in this network are reading *Mein Kampf*, *The Turner Diaries*, and works of Julius Evola and Savitri Devi, George Lincoln Rockwell, and James Mason, and so on. In other words, these are not new sources nor from the standpoint of Nazism or white supremacist movements historically would they be considered fringe or heterodox. This is *fascist canon*. It's exactly what you'd expect them to be reading, to the point of stereotype.

There are some reasons why people might think the skullmask accelerationists specifically are not "ideological." I will consider and respond to some possible reasons for this claim.

First, people might say that because accelerationism sees any kind of chaos as good, it cannot be an ideology. That misses the point. Fascist accelerationism has a very clear goal: a world fascist empire and the genocide of various groups, especially Jews. Chaos is a necessary component in the cycle through which it believes history resets itself. Belief in the power of destructive remaking has *always* been at the heart of fascist ideology.

Another reason people might see accelerationists as lacking an ideology is that foundational recent texts like those of Slavros insist that accelerationism is not an ideology, and many members of the skullmask network have read his texts and commit to not calling fascism an ideology. "People would get very mad at you in the group if you called it an ideology," a former skullmask told me.[20] But the reasons why the skullmasks rejected the term "ideology" were not about a lack of concern for the specificity of worldviews but for different reasons:

- First, IronMarch founder Slavros wrote that fascism was and must be described as *the* Truth (capital T) and that calling fascism an "ideology" reduced it to merely one perspective among many.[21] This is obviously not a claim we are required to take seriously. Any cult leader, likewise, might say, "This isn't a religion. This is just the truth," and those of us not in the cult would just say, "Okay, then. Interesting religion you've got there." Obviously, this is a convenient belief for those who want to prevent dialogue, doubt, or syncretism: if one's own belief system is "the Truth" and all other belief systems are mere "ideology," then one's beliefs are beyond question and kept "pure" from outside intrusion. But to nonbelievers in the particular ideology, such claims are meaningless.

- Second, we also see in the foundational writings by Slavros that he wanted to insist that fascism was not an ideology because "ideology" sounded narrowly political, and he wanted to stress fascism's "philosophical" aspects and thus preferred the term "worldview."[22] But ideologies, and the social movements through which they find life, are *often* not a narrow political program. Anarchism and socialism, for example, are not about a narrow set of political aims but are also philosophies and visions for a new world, a new society, and new or renewed ways of human relating. Yet most people would agree that anarchism and socialism are "ideologies" under the broad definition I offered earlier.
- Third, there were members of Atomwaffen who discussed among themselves the formation of a "coalitional accelerationism." Likely, the use of this specific term by counter-extremism researchers is related to its first usage in that context, whether in the course of observing online discussions among accelerationists or in interviewing former accelerationists. However, far from a sign of caring about their beliefs less than usual, skullmask "coalitional accelerationism" seems to be another tactic of deception, a means to infiltrate and take over other movements and subcultures to promote particular views or amplify conflict, chaos, and violence.

Besides the hostility of the movement itself to the term "ideology," there are a few other reasons one might want to say this network is not "ideological." These are (1) the internet-based nature of its organizing; (2) the presence of the elusive and ideologically confusing Satanist network, O9A, among the skullmasks; and (3) the anti-rational, anti-philosophical side of fascism itself. As we shall see, none of these rationales are sufficient to ascribe a non- or post-ideological character to the skullmask network.

1 The Role of the Internet

First, certain observations, and combined with certain starting assumptions about the implications of internet-based mobilization, might lead one to see accelerationism as a process of moving past ideology. In particular, the use of online platform Telegram by accelerationists to organize, post memes, and desensitize recruits to violence has received a lot of attention. That the same memes are sometimes used across different ideological tendencies, especially on Telegram by Nazis and supporters of ISIS, has also received much attention. I suspect some researchers' fascination with this is enhanced by the grouping of both "terrorist" threats under the same heading of "extremism," with considerable access to grant money and government contacts entailed in seeing all the enemies of Western neoliberalism as in some kind of alliance with one another. (More on this problem of analysis in Chapter 4.) However, hate has been online since the early 1980s, and white supremacists like Don Black, the creator of the Stormfront website, a longtime hub for white supremacist organizing, have been using and discussing the importance of the internet for mobilizing their movements since at least the 1990s.[23]

Furthermore, new modalities of organizing, even new tactics, do not in themselves imply new ideologies nor a breakdown of ideological allegiance. The latest attempts to theorize shifts in fascist mobilization should not take us astray into believing there has been a diminution of fascist ideology (specifically at a moment when I would argue it is encountering resurgence!). There have long been attempts to rename or classify postwar fascist organizing that stressed new social formations and employed a variety of metaphors and analogies.

There is some truth to the internet leading to new forms of organizing and attack by the alt-right. New formations seem to be emerging, such as the alt-right's action as a web-based "swarm."[24] The alt-right was partly born out of campaigns of online harassment beginning on websites 4chan and Reddit in 2014, first with divisive racist tweets pretending to be Black feminists canceling Father's Day[25] and then with the so-called Gamergate attacks, in which male video gamers harassed and attacked female critics of sexism in video games. It is difficult to overestimate the lasting harm of such campaigns, including targets being subjected to doxxing (posting of their addresses, sometimes pictures of their homes, and other personal information online) and the overwhelming numbers of death and explicit rape threats. There was not only a degree of coordination in these activities but also trolls who simply joined the bullies' feeding frenzy. Internet trolling and mobbing are often not coordinated, with the targets arrived at almost by chance, as the growing multitude of attacks seem to "swarm" like bees over them. Like a many-headed hydra, the swarm does not have a single strategy yet converges on its victims and locales.[26] Fascists and the alt-right specifically were and are only part of this swarm but an essential part.[27]

Before the rise of the alt-right and before Nazis gathered on Telegram, Roger Griffin argued in a 2003 article that fascist mobilization should be interpreted as forming into "groupuscules,"[28] or "myriad minute, and at times highly ephemeral and eminently unmemorable grouplets."[29] Griffin drew on Deleuze and Guattari's image of the "rhizome," a subterranean network of interconnected plant roots, to suggest that the contemporary fascist movements can be seen as "cellular, centerless and leaderless network with ill-defined boundaries and no formal hierarchy or internal organizational structure."[30] To Deleuze and Guattari's rhizome, Griffin added his own category of the slime mold: "a hybrid life-form made up of countless single-cell organisms" that "has no central nervous system [yet]…somehow moves purposefully."[31]

Expanding on the analyses offered by Griffin and Deleuze and Guattari, in his recent book *On Microfascism*, Jack Bratich distinguishes between "squads" and "groupuscules," suggesting that fascist vigilantism now takes the form of groupuscules rather than squads.[32] Unlike far-right death squads, Italian fascist squadrismo, and organized militias, there is a different kind of social formation emerging to prominence that Bratich argues lacks even the level of organization found in the structure of small coordinated violent "cells" of a larger organization and that might be better characterized on the groupuscular model.[33]

In short, I suggest, fascist ideology has not changed in epistemic structure or ideological content due to new technologies but is simply mobilizing in new ways in line with its longtime epistemological and ideological commitments. These various categorizations have long attempted to show the ways in which fascist organizing spreads, networks, and mutates. Looking for the most accurate categories, metaphors, and analogies to describe shifting forms of fascist mobilization is not an unimportant exercise, because how we picture fascism shapes how we fight it. But the constant rise of trendy new terms can deceive us into believing we are encountering an entirely new monster when we are not. Innovative approaches and new discoveries get grant money and media attention, but staying grounded in traditions of antifascist analysis and movement-building is more crucial for defeating this ongoing and resurgent fascist threat.

2 Order of Nine Angles

Another, and perhaps the most difficult issue, concerns the influence or intersection of the O9A on the skullmask movement. O9A is an international Satanist network that professes the "left-hand path," the more "sinister" and conniving side of Satanism. O9A even advocates human sacrifice ("culling") as a means of transcending the commitments of the Jewish and Christian faiths, or what they call "Magianism."[34] O9A also advocates for followers to adopt "insight roles" in groups, social movements, or institutions, spending at least a year in an "identity, career, religion, or an ideology that is opposite to the follower's belief or character," such as joining a "leftist extremist" group, the police, or converting to Islam.[35] Speculations as to O9A's deeper intentions or how far its infiltration of particular institutions has reached are beyond this book's scope, but the connections between O9A and Nazism are not recent to O9A's development nor tangential. According to U.K. group Hope Not Hate, "The Order of Nine Angles is intrinsically intertwined with Nazism."[36] From Hope Not Hate (Nick Lowles):

> When asked in 2005 if the O9A were posing as nazis to recruit and spread their message, Myatt...responded: You seem to have missed the point about ONA and National Socialism. "From the get-go the ONA have propagated holocaust revisionism, have praised Hitler, have encouraged members to join NS [National Socialist, Nazi] groups."

Myatt also stressed to Hope Not Hate that one of the "core principles" of the Order of Nine Angles was opposition to Magianism, and that "Magian is ONA code for ZOG," or the "Zionist Occupation Government," which Hope Not Hate explains is "a phrase to describe the Jewish control of the state that became widely adopted by nazis in the 1980s and 90s."[37]

While its tendency to take on "insight roles" suggests that O9A might be more ideologically complex than some Nazi groups, it clearly is "intertwined" with Nazism. The presence of O9A within the skullmask network, at any rate, is not sufficient in my view to see the skullmask network as anything less than ideologically motivated by fascism and Nazism, as the skullmasks' own documents (which I discuss later in this chapter) make clear.

3   Fascism's Anti-Ideological Character

One might also, from an external and critical standpoint, call fascism anti-ideological because of the ways in which it is hostile to rationality. It resists argumentation since it believes that truth is merely intuitively known to those who are superior and destined to rule and that truth is also in some way *created* by their powerful, mythic action. It also rejects clear political programs, since its vision of change is, again, *destructive and mythic* rather than an organized process. Peruvian Marxist José Carlos Mariátegui rightly wrote that fascism is fundamentally "not a concept" because of this quality of irrationality.[38] Adorno, again, wrote of "vagueness with regard to political aims...inherent in Fascism itself" and of fascism's "intrinsically untheoretical nature."[39] However, to call fascism "anti-ideological" because of this would likely generate confusion, and since this is not a new feature of fascism, there is no case to be made on this basis that fascist accelerationists are currently becoming less ideological.

Understanding fascism as an ideology helps us to challenge the reductivism of the thesis of coalitional accelerationism. If ideology no longer matters for accelerationism, those studying accelerationism can focus their attention on government-sponsored prevention programs and policing—political analysis and activism become irrelevant. But if fascism (including in its current "accelerationist" formations) is an ideology and a social movement seeking power, as I argue here, it must be fought with countervailing social movements. Activism and political analysis (in the sense of left analysis of present conditions, not a narrow investigation of political parties and policy) remain necessary.

Instead of tracking mere behavior or opposition to the government and the status quo of American values and institutions (free markets, etc.), I suggest that we study the accelerationist impulse as a prime expression of fascism itself, as I am doing in this chapter. Although non-fascists can embrace accelerationist thinking, fascism is inherently accelerationist in a way that many other belief systems are not. In fact, the inherently destructive nature of fascism has long been an object of study. In the Frankfurt School, Adorno, Fromm, and others wrote on the phenomenon. Adorno, for example, wrote that,

> [fascist] programs are abstract and vague, the fulfillments are spurious and illusory because the promise expressed by fascist oratory is nothing but destruction itself. It is hardly accidental that all fascist agitators dwell upon the imminence of catastrophes of some kind.[40]

Later in this chapter, I explore how accelerationist visions of change have been promoted through a fascist mythology that appropriates from Hindu concepts of cyclical time.

Prophetic and Catastrophic: Two Kinds of Yearning for Total Transformation

We need to think about different approaches to revolutionary transformation and the emotional impulses or states of individual character that drive them. This will help us see how fascist destructiveness differs from genuine leftist revolutionary impulses in ways that overgeneralizations about "extremism" or "radicalism" fail to capture. A distinction drawn from Critical Theory may be helpful here: Erich Fromm distinguished between a revolutionary kind of socialist utopian hope he called "prophetic messianism" and a more desperate approach to social change, called "catastrophic messianism," which saw instigating social disorder as the only way to make change. Much of Fromm's work constitutes a defense of prophetic messianism and a critique of catastrophic messianism, and Fromm's critique of catastrophic messianism contained a critique of fascist visions of time and destruction.

"Messianism" here is a term taken from the Jewish tradition, where the question of the "Messiah" refers not to a person or a god but to a coming *time* that would fulfill human hopes for justice, freedom, and peace: the long-awaited "messianic age." For socialist and anarchist Jewish radical intellectuals in 1920s Germany, "messianism" also constituted a political term of debate; the messianism debate concerned the nature of revolutionary or reformist change and the philosophy of history. Avant-garde Jewish intellectuals like Erich Fromm, Martin Buber, Gershom Scholem, Franz Rosenzweig, Walter Benjamin, and Ernst Bloch, in their writings on "messianism," knew they were asking a political question. That is, how does the hoped-for future (e.g., socialism) come to be? Does it require mysterious transcendent forces (God or human leaders) intervening to rescue a fallen humanity? Or can the coming "messianic age" arrive (as some Jewish theologians believed) as the product of human beings actively choosing to construct a new future together?

"Prophetic messianism" is a *radical hope* for the messianic future, grounded in a faith in humanity's potential to bring it about. "Hope," for Fromm, is active—actively engaged in the work of bringing about its desired future. This is the work of social movements, in which individuals play the role of the organizer or "prophet," who rallies the public by making people aware of the critical juncture at which they find themselves and presenting the "alternatives" between which they must choose. (Fromm offers famous German Marxist revolutionary and theoretician Rosa Luxemburg as an example of a "prophet" offering "alternatives," with her famous call on the eve of the rise of fascism for humanity to choose quickly between "socialism or barbarism.") Prophetic messianism is also grounded in a "paradoxical" understanding that, although one must have faith in humanity's future, human beings also have agency and can choose destruction. History does not operate according to inexorable laws and will not force a particular outcome, so if human beings want to destroy the world and end all of history in calamity—by ecological destruction, economic collapse, annihilation in war, or the abandonment of humanistic ideals in favor of widespread fascist and chauvinistic nationalist movements—that is also a choice within our power.

In his *Letter from Birmingham Jail*, Rev. Dr. Martin Luther King, Jr. plays a similar prophetic function to the one Fromm describes, calling on people to act quickly and urgently for an end to racist segregation. Like Fromm, King critiques passive waiting. Responding to white clergy who objected that King's activism was "unwise and untimely," King argues against the constantly repeated demands that Black people "wait" for a more acceptable time to take action, arguing that "justice too long delayed is justice denied" and critiquing what he calls the "mythical concept of time," according to which justice would arrive at a foreordained time without human effort.[41]

Prophetic messianism is revolutionary, not reformist: it does not believe that the messianic age is a product of cataclysm, but it does believe that it is only through revolutionary change, not patching up the current system, that the messianic age becomes a possibility. It is a notion of revolutionary hope that is highly attuned to potential. Fromm believed that the radical hope of prophetic messianism had almost been defeated with World War I and the 1919 assassinations of socialist leader Rosa Luxemburg and anarchist leader Gustav Landauer, both Jewish revolutionaries who stood up to nationalism and for working-class solidarity.[42] Luxemburg and Landauer, according to Fromm, were "prophets" in the sense of recognizing the nature of the moment facing them and calling upon people to understand the crucial juncture at which history was standing and to make the correct choice. Rosa Luxemburg's theory of the "mass strike" reflected a deep understanding that history is made not through transcendent interventions but through the somewhat unpredictable emergence of uprisings that occur when the people are ready to move. Gustav Landauer's vision of anarchist revolution similarly rests on his understanding that when revolutionary transformation occurs, it is not so much a bolt of lightning from above but something that grows up from within the present, through the construction of new structures: "Appealing to the people" is insufficient, Landauer writes; instead we must "show others and ourselves what socialism means *in action*. We must realize as much of socialism as possible *right here and right now*."[43]

"Catastrophic messianism," which Fromm opposed, believes that the messianic age arrives when transcendent forces intervene into history at the moment of humanity's greatest weakness and collapse. According to this view, the small and large gains of social movements are not a sign that the messianic age is coming—rather, things have to get a whole lot worse before they can get better, and mysterious forces (human, natural, or divine) will intervene to direct humanity into the messianic age when things get bad enough. Catastrophic messianism takes two forms: passive and active. If catastrophe can lead to the messianic age, then only two pathways are possible: (1) waiting, rising above history to a kind of spiritual placidity while awaiting salvation or (2) "forcing the time," in which one attempts by means of some kind of disruption, chaos, or violence, to worsen history in order to semi-magically reset it.

The two forms of catastrophic messianism—passivity and forcing the time—are related. Drawing on Aristotle's ethics, Fromm would have seen virtues as existing between two vices characterized by some kind of excess. For example, a person who has the virtue of honesty avoids both dishonesty and unnecessary bluntness or indiscretion, or a person who has the virtue of courage, likewise, avoids both cowardice and recklessness in the face of danger. If "prophetic messianism" is a virtue of healthy hopefulness, it too exists between two extremes: *passive resignation* (the "waiting" condemned by King) and impulse to "destroy the world to save it" (in the words of Robert Jay Lifton's famous book on the terroristic Aum Shinrikyo cult). And as with the vices opposed to any virtue, these two impulses of passivity and destructiveness are more related to each other than they are to hope. Each is caused by a similar belief about the powerlessness of humanity to effect change and the inscrutable laws that govern human history.

Prophetic messianism is a virtue of political hope. Aristotle also believed that the two opposed vices were more alike each other than the virtuous mean. If we think about hope more generally, virtue ethicists in the Middle Ages (namely, the Catholic philosopher Saint Thomas Aquinas) situated hope between the twin extremes of despair and presumption. Whether one is *despairing* of salvation's possibility or *presuming* one will achieve it effortlessly, one no longer has to try to be good—one's agency has no impact on one's future possibilities. Similarly, Fromm writes in his late book on fascist destructiveness, *The Anatomy of Human Destructiveness*, that optimism and pessimism are very alike: the optimist believes that nothing *needs* to be done, and the pessimist that nothing *can* be done.[44]

Fascism is one expression—perhaps the pre-eminent expression—of catastrophic messianism. As such, fascism embraces both passivity and forcing the time ("destroying the world to save it"). For all its promises of paving the way to a new world, there is something inherently despairing, and hence desperate, in fascism. (Trotsky, similarly to Fromm, had contrasted communism as the "party of revolutionary hope" to fascism as "the party of counter-revolutionary despair."[45]) In what follows, I explore how fascist ideology, in some of its historic and contemporary manifestations, incorporates both passive despair and destructiveness. Both tendencies are linked to a cyclical vision of history, which believes that things *must* get worse in order to get better. According to fascist ideology, as we shall see, history operates according to inexorable laws of rise and decline, and while at times one may have to simply wait ("ride the tiger," in Evola's terms), fascists believe that, in other times, heroic individuals can create and then manage the worsening of societal conditions necessary for history to return to its higher points. Enraged, egotistical, and covering over their deep self-doubt with their pride in their movement and their race, fascists go to war to recreate the world according to their image. They come to believe that the world is wholly rotten and deserves to be destroyed, and they rationalize this destruction as creation, while also part of set laws of nature or history, and as the only way that the past hierarchies they desire can be restored and renewed.

Catastrophism, Dehumanization, and Eliminationism

Fascism's nihilistic, catastrophic-messianic approach to history arises in part from its dehumanization of others. Because fascism views its scapegoats, and ultimately all human beings, as having no inherent dignity or worth, fascism views human beings as disposable. This dehumanization, in turn, is grounded in the belief that violence and injustice are the ways of the world and must simply be embraced; instead of trying to improve the world, they believe, the fascist should seek to be on the winning team.

In *Prophets of Deceit* (Leo Lowenthal's study of the American antisemitic "agitator" mentioned in Chapter 1), Lowenthal finds the rhetoric of the fascist antisemitic "agitator" reflects a belief that the inherent injustice of the world cannot be defeated, only embraced. He suggests that the antisemitic agitator is asking audiences to join with a powerful winning team (with the "police" against the "prisoners"). According to Lowenthal, it is the "malaise" and "homelessness" of the disaffected that drives them to fascism (again, "filling the void"), more than any conviction about the tenets of the ideology. In this malaise, which fascism cannot salve, "the individual lives in a sort of eternal adolescent uneasiness."[46] The fascist promises their followers protection from the dangers and uncertainty of "the hostile world." In exchange for the warm embrace of the authoritarian leader and fellow followers, the follower must submit to the agitator and profess by their actions a belief in life's meaninglessness, learning to see power and force as life's only arbiters. In exchange for submission and the acceptance of a philosophy of violent nihilism, the follower receives the agitator's protection and approval and gets to join the bullies, becoming a victimizer rather than a victim, in what they believe to be the inevitable race for power that defines all human life. To use an image that became popular on the alt-right, fascism conceives the world along the lines of the choice in a "zombie apocalypse" film: kill the zombie or become the zombie. Violence constitutes the fascist recruit's only concept of the possibility of survival for the people or the race. Issuing what Lowenthal calls a "call to the hunt" against the scapegoated enemy, the agitator simultaneously professes the inevitability of the enemy's demise. Like all others who stand against the tide, the victim (the Jew, in the case of Lowenthal's antisemitic agitator) will inevitably be crushed by reality's inescapable violence and injustice: "They must be liquidated because they are doomed" is the fascists' attitude—"there is no place for the individual in the world today," they believe.[47]

At the conclusion of the book, Lowenthal and Guterman offer a "translation" of the fascist agitator's rhetoric:

> My friends, we live in a world of inequality and injustice. But whoever believes that this state of affairs will ever be or can ever be changed is a fool or a liar. Oppression and injustice, as war and famine, are eternal accompaniments of human life. The idealists who claim otherwise are merely fooling themselves—and worse still, are merely fooling you. To indulge in gestures of human brotherhood is merely bait for suckers.[48]

The fascist agitator then offers protection to those who join the bullies: "We will form an iron-bound movement of terror. We will ally ourselves with the powerful in order to gain part of their privilege. We will be the policemen rather than the prisoners."[49] Accepting that anyone who seeks to evade the world's violent nature is fated for defeat, and accepting their fate as conquerors, fascist recruits undertake a war against outsiders.

The belief that the "natural order" of the world involves injustice and that "might makes right" is explicitly expressed by the skullmask accelerationists. Slavros's short story *A Squire's Trial*, co-authored with another fascist, romanticizes fascism as a mysterious quest, a hero's journey, and a philosophical enterprise. (The short story was a required text for new members of Atomwaffen Division, who were required to pass a quiz on it along with some other texts.) The hero is a swashbuckling, ever-confident globe-trotter who preaches the principle that "might makes right." He promises to teach his new recruit the one universal, capital-T "Truth" that he says all fascists seek and is embedded in nature itself, which turns out to be this:

> Our whole existence is filled with suffering, with pain. No matter what we do, we can't change that fact, no matter what laws we make or what social order we adopt. The only thing we can change, is WHO suffers, and in WHAT way.

This is the fundamental "truth" at which fascism arrives and on which it is based. Fascism is a fundamental surrender in the effort to improve the world, choosing instead to redistribute suffering. Although at the surface level of its propaganda, fascism appears to be attempting to create a better world, it is also based on the belief that injustice is natural and not undesirable.

Slavros articulates the same claim in *Next Leap*, an anthology of essays on fascism that members of Atomwaffen Division were also required to read.[50] Slavros equates morality with what he calls "the natural order," which he distinguishes from a morality based on respect for human dignity. At his most blunt, he states, "We don't think murder is wrong, and we do not believe that every human life is sacred. This applies to our own people as well."[51]

Despite how blunt some fascist groups may be about their rejection of human dignity and their embrace of injustice, they nevertheless always engage in some self-deception and subterfuge about what they are doing and what their movement represents. The image of the fascist bully is covered over with romanticizations and notions of heroism, as we saw earlier, for example, in James Mason's depiction of the nobility of the "lone wolf." In *Squire's Trial*, for example, the fascist hero who teaches fascism to his young recruit is romanticized as a wanderer, a "pirate," a mysterious figure with "stories to tell."

The partly unconscious awareness that fascism is a form of despairing bullying—that fascism is grounded in the belief that the world is irrevocably unjust, and the fascist simply wants to be on the winning team, to be the bully rather than the bullied, to be the "dog-eater" rather than the "dog-eaten" in a dog-eat-dog world—is psychologically nearly impossible for the fascist to face. This is not necessarily because the fascist wants to be perceived as good and kind, by themselves or others—many may not particularly care. Rather, the fascist hides from awareness of their own vulnerability and from the knowledge that the fascist's beliefs may not be the "natural" products of an innate, superior racial intuition but merely a psychological defense mechanism to protect the fascist's emotional weakness. Consequently, this reality is covered over by further defense mechanisms, including particular discourses and acts of violence. By violently forcing reality to fit a preconceived notion of truth, the identity of the fascist is protected: as a winner, by nature. In this manner, fascists can at least temporarily protect their fragile sense of personal identity, the idol with which they fill their personal voids.

Dehumanization is part of the process of the fascist forcing reality to accord with their preconceived notions and sense of self. The other is sometimes perceived as somehow *already dead*, like the zombie, which also makes violence and genocide easier to justify. In her discussion of the Nazi genocide of mental hospital patients, Claudia Leeb notes the role of "code names": those with disabilities were classified as living "unlivable lives," as not fully living, and their deaths as not really killing ("euthanasia" or "sleeping peacefully across").[52] Fascism cannot acknowledge its victims—when it is tempted to do so, fascism presents itself as the eternal victim and its violence as self-defense against enemies depicted as undead, non-human hordes. (Fascism blames its victims, following the DARVO pattern employed by bullies and abusers: Deny, Attack, and Reverse Victim and Offender.[53])

At the same time, however, fascism is always already aware of the humanity of its victims and must constantly repress this awareness. Systematic dehumanization *always* requires knowing and then systematically denying the humanity of the other, an insight embodied in Hegel's "master-slave dialectic." The colonizer, the slaveholder, the concentration camp guard, and the racist skinhead curb-stomping a hapless victim are all aware on some level of the humanity of those they harm, at the very moment in which they violently dehumanize them. They know they are harming human beings, even as they claim to be simply cleaning up the world, Christianizing it, furthering progress or science, or ridding the world of "vermin" or "infections."

Perhaps no one more effectively laid out this phenomenon of the reliance of dehumanization on prior recognition of the humanity of the other than the Black abolitionist leader, philosopher, and orator Frederick Douglass. In fact, dehumanization is arguably the central theme of his work, including his famous *Narrative of the Life of Frederick Douglass* and his 1852 address, "Is the Slave a Man?": "Must I undertake to prove that the slave is a man? That point is conceded already. Nobody doubts it. The slaveholders themselves acknowledge it in the enactment of laws for their government."[54]

The slaveholder denies enslaved persons education because the slaveholder understands all too well the power of education to awaken human hopes and provide tools for liberation. The slaveholder denies the enslaved person their family connections and even a knowledge of the enslaved persons' own birthdates, knowing the power of a human being who has a strong sense of personal identity. The slaveholder keeps the enslaved person half-naked, hungry, brutalized, and afraid, in an attempt to prevent them from grasping and fighting for their own humanity—and to insulate the slaveholder from having to face the full reality of the harm they are doing to other human beings.

The rhetoric of dehumanization can easily shift between targets or be expanded to apply to new "others." It is not static in its choice of scapegoats. For example, during the COVID-19 pandemic, there was a spike in anti-Asian hate crimes. We also now see, for example, how dehumanization is being increasingly directed against transgender people as of this writing and also, in the process, an apparent increase in open expression of vitriolic homophobia. Meanwhile, the reaction against trans rights is going on in the area of policy, with numerous states passing bans on gender-affirming care for minors, on allowing trans people to use the bathrooms with which they identify, and on drag shows, mischaracterized as inherently sexual and "sexualizing" of children. I want to draw attention here to one other group against which dehumanization and eliminationism also seem to be rising: the unhoused.

Questioned by a bystander after appearing to veer dangerously onto a sidewalk in pursuit of a suspect, a Seattle police officer defended himself against those who wanted to defund the police and added, "I used to love Seattle…It's pretty fucking dirty." Expert on far-right extremism David Neiwert tweeted that the cop's actions and comments seemed to represent "eliminationism," a phenomenon Neiwert has studied.[55] The cop's statement seemed to imply that since Seattle is "dirty," it no longer deserves protection. Neiwert defines eliminationism as a politics that seeks the "suppression, exile, ejection, or extermination" of its enemies and that

> depicts its opposition as beyond the pale, the embodiment of evil itself, unfit for participation in their vision of society, and thus worthy of elimination. It often further depicts its designated Enemy as vermin (especially rats and cockroaches) or diseases, and disease-like cancers on the body politic.[56]

The eliminationism found in Nazi ideology is "extreme" only in a relative sense and is reflected in mainstream propaganda like pro-small business, pro-police, anti-homeless television documentary *Seattle Is Dying*, which I suspect may have influenced the attitude of the Seattle cop who no longer loved

Seattle. Released in March 2019, *Seattle Is Dying* focused on the growing unhoused population in Seattle and presented drug use as the cause of homelessness. The film is primarily a petty-bourgeois plea for law and order through the rounding up and confinement of the unhoused, whom it argues should be incarcerated and forced to undergo drug addiction treatment. The film portrayed the unhoused as "animals" and dirty, needing to be caged (incarcerated) to protect police, tourists, and shopkeepers. The film participated in the fascist tropes of scapegoating an "other" as dirty, diseased, and subhuman, even issuing a kind of "call to the hunt" (to use Lowenthal's term). From the film:

> They use deadly drugs, and they sell those drugs for ten bucks a dose. And over and over, they steal us blind to get the ten bucks. And they pollute our streets and parks and neighborhoods, and they live in filth and despair, like animals. And we allow it—all of it. We used to talk about "compassion."

Seattle Is Dying is mirrored by the broader activities of petty-bourgeois fascism: the defense of property easily slips into intimidation and even vigilantism, with accompanying dehumanizing rhetoric. When we look to the historical progenitors of fascist or proto-fascist groups like the Proud Boys today, we should include the actions of groups of enraged veterans and strikebreakers after World War I attacking "Wobblies," socialist offices, and striking workers, their nativism and xenophobia expressing itself as a reactionary, counter-revolutionary politics. Eliminationism lurks within the mainstream, and when those being eliminated are already too marginalized even for large social movements to be likely to mobilize in their defense, eliminationist policies can be carried on simultaneously with a mainstream politics that counterposes itself to "extremism."

Fascist dehumanization conceives its scapegoated enemies as waste to be eliminated, but this involves a degree of projection, an attempt to annihilate something outside the self that the fascist is evading internally. An aspect of this is the projection of the fascist's own sense of vulnerability or weakness onto its scapegoated enemies, whom it nevertheless must perceive as strong and formidable, both to sustain its vision of itself as a heroic warrior and to sustain its belief in its own victimhood.

In their study of the antisemitic (fascist) agitator, Lowenthal and Guterman wrote that the agitator hates the Jew for being both strong and weak. The Jew's strength is jealously despised: the Jew is "at home in every country" and "has solved the problem of belonging"; "although he is an individual, he is never isolated. And he shapes his own fate...both his own and the other nations' fates."[57] At the same time, the Jew is viewed as a victim who, like all others who stand against the tide, will be crushed inevitably by reality's inescapable violence and injustice.[58] The belief in the fundamental injustice of the world and the absence of any possibility of justice—violence and harm as the "natural order"—is part and parcel of the fascist's decision to annihilate the other.

Fascist and far-right movements in the United States today continue to perceive their enemies as a whole as both weak (to assist nature or fate in crushing) and strong (to be jealously despised). The enemy is weak: "snowflakes" and "cucks," emotionally fragile and "triggered," "betas," effete intellectuals, "low IQ," and "basic." But the enemy is also strong: the "globalist" elite manipulator, the Social Justice Warrior, the "terrorist" Antifa, or "violent" Black Lives Matter member in the pay of (Jewish) George Soros or underwritten by the supposedly wide-ranging Frankfurt School Jewish conspiracy of "cultural Marxism" that they believe to control the universities and wider culture.[59]

But just as the scapegoated victim is perceived as both strong (dangerous) and weak (destined to be crushed), so too is the fascist agitator bound by this dual identity; the fascist's perception of the other is a projection of her own blend of strength and weakness, Lowenthal finds. Lowenthal's agitator brags about his insider knowledge and ability while complaining about the difficulties of being an agitator and stressing the sacrifices that he has made for the cause. In this manner, the fascist constructs an identity as both strong hero and persecuted martyr.[60]

The enemy's weakness is proof to the fascist that the enemy's destiny is annihilation. To be "weak" is to be fated for annihilation in the coming conflict. In "higher" periods of historical cycles, the fascist believes, perhaps the "weak" would be assigned a subordinate (e.g., enslaved) position in a social hierarchy. But since this social order is not possible on the downward slope of a historical cycle, the enemy must primarily be eliminated in order to make way for a new social order. Dehumanization is thus inherently linked to the historical cycle of destruction and rebirth.

Destruction and Rebirth

Fascism has always involved a particular vision of time. It identifies the present as the low point in a cyclical vision of history: a present of decline or "degeneration." Return to the high point requires the intervention of heroic individuals and movements, they believe, and including eventually a mythic leader, to reset history. Although fascism tends to view the historical cycle as partly predetermined—thus, it is a pessimistic ideology that downplays human potential and agency—fascism also believes that *how* the cycle regenerates can be controlled to some degree. That is, there is flexibility in terms of how and when the cycle returns to its "high" point. A final apocalyptic destruction may even end the cycle forever if the cycle is not managed properly. They believe *destructive remaking* is needed for the cycle to return from decline to ascendancy. The present must be violently destabilized, and the new hierarchically ordered world must be rebuilt on new foundations.

Importantly, this destructiveness is not caused only by fascism's desire for the world to be *dramatically otherwise*. The core of fascism's destructive vision lies in its belief that change results semi-magically (mystically, mythically) from destruction. Destruction is not viewed as a mere tactical necessity, in this view, to make room for something new to be constructed. Rather, it is believed that destruction itself—violence itself—restores and renews. Thus, fascism is at its core a version of "catastrophic messianism," seeing salvation as possible only through catastrophe and the intervention of mysterious transcendent forces (mythic heroes), not through the constructive agency of human beings at large.

Roger Griffin famously identified fascism as "palingenetic," as committed to a kind of destructive and mythic rebirth of a people.[61] Griffin sees fascism as ideological, about reclaiming "mythological identity and order."[62] Without taking a position on whether Griffin's definition of fascism is the best one, one can see that Griffin's definition brings forward an aspect of the dynamic I am addressing in this chapter. "Palingenesis" (rebirth) suggests both a past to return to and a new reality to create. This attempt to both return and create anew is central to fascism's cyclical vision of history. And a birth is messy (painful for the one who gives birth), different from a gradual evolution. Although a vision of destruction and rebirth is shared by many ideologies, Griffin argues that fascism tends to differ in the way that it places palingenesis as its core inspiring myth; fascism is more enraptured by palingenesis itself than by a vision of the sort of society it wants to build after the apocalyptic collapse.[63]

Kali-Yuga

Fascism's belief in a historical cycle of destruction and remaking has often involved a fascination with Hindu cosmology and its theory of the "Kali-yuga." Fascist writers appropriated the concept of the Kali-yuga from Hinduism to describe their vision of the complete "degeneracy" of present society and their expectation of a coming mythic leader who would destroy and reset the world. The Hindu sacred text, the *Bhagavad Gita*, describes the god Krishna returning cyclically, age after age, to reset history and to "restore dharma," to restore virtue, reverence, and social order. The particular avatar (expression) of Krishna that returns to end the Kali-yuga is known in Hinduism as "Kalki." Hinduism, as one of the great world religions, of course, should not be equated with the beliefs of the Nazis who appropriate it. This also applies to the human rights violations of the Modi regime in

India today or the hateful rhetoric of some Hindu nationalist movements, on which there are fascist influences. The same rationality and courtesy typically given of distinguishing Christianity from Christian nationalist/fascist iterations, for example, should be extended here to Hinduism.

Julius Evola (1898–1974) and Savitri Devi (1905–1982) were two prominent fascist writers who appropriated the Hindu concept of the Kali-yuga and the return of Kalki to restore dharma; their writings continue to be influential on contemporary fascist movements. Keep these concepts in mind as we proceed, because I am also outlining this theory here to set the stage for my discussion of Steve Bannon in the next chapter; Bannon also was influenced by reactionary theories appropriating the Kali-yuga to articulate the need for a catastrophic "turning" and remaking of history.

Italian fascist and occultist writer Julius Evola belonged to the "Traditionalist School," a group of thinkers founded early in the twentieth century that continues as a loose network or set of networks today, and which has occultist and neo-pagan influences as well as some historical and contemporary ties to fascism. "Traditionalism," capital T, is a reactionary, anti-Enlightenment school of thought that includes alongside Evola founding figures such as René Guénon (1886–1951), Frithjof Schuon (1907–1998), and Mircea Eliade (1907–1986).

Traditionalists believe that multiple religions share a secret content known only to elite initiates, not the majority of believers. They tend to believe that this secret content, predating the Abrahamic faiths, can be accessed through the practice of a particular tradition with an eye to its "hidden" meaning.

Rather than evolving or making progress, "Traditions," as understood by thinkers like Guénon, are a site of return to a deep mythical and pre-rational human past. History is conceived as an eternal return to unchanging buried truths, a cycle of remembering and forgetting. Furthermore, the preservation of and return to Tradition are seen as connected to preserving or restoring social hierarchies. The small spiritual elite that grasps the hidden truth uniting traditions is tasked with special roles in preserving or restoring this hierarchy. Traditionalists see hierarchy as fundamental to a sense of meaning, favor the idea of social "castes," see modernity and the Enlightenment as marking a decline in civilization, and are highly skeptical of democracy. According to Traditionalism's cyclic view of human history, the collapse of modernity and democracy is coming soon, inaugurating a new Golden Age of hierarchy and obedience. This cannot occur gradually—according to Traditionalism's catastrophic messianism, things have to get maximally "bad" before they can get maximally "better."

Appropriating a four-part Hindu cosmology, Traditionalists like Guénon and Evola believed that the current dark age known in Hindu cosmology as the Kali-yuga[64] would be ending soon, returning human history to a thousands-year-long Golden Age (or Satya-yuga). Since the Nazis believed that Aryans were originally from India, they appropriated elements of Hindu mysticism, this cosmology among them. (The most famous Nazi symbol, the swastika, was also adapted from the Eastern religion.) The Kali-yuga is characterized by all the sorts of things one would expect in an age of decline: natural disasters, poor health, immorality. But a crucial sign that the Kali-yuga is nearing its end is a reversal of social roles: those who should be priestly Brahmins act like servants, and servants act like Brahmins, i.e., a reversal of social roles and of the hierarchy of values, a phenomenon that René Guénon called "inversion." No doubt defenders of societal hierarchies are attracted to the idea of a coming Golden Age that they see as reversing gains in equality, returning or securing the oppressed to their subservient "place" in the social hierarchy and restoring "priestly" rule.

At the end of the Kali-yuga, according to the Hindu cosmology, an avatar of the god Vishnu, named Kalki, returns to lead humanity to a new Golden Age. The Hindu cosmology also posits cycles within cycles: there are thus smaller cycles within each part of the cycle, such as rises and declines within the Kali-yuga itself. Preceding Kalki, other avatars arrive throughout the Kali-yuga to point toward its end, so within the Kali-yuga, a series of appearances of the god arrive to lead the smaller cycles back from decline to high point. After the cycle of four yugas has been completed many times over, according to this belief system, the world itself is destroyed and re-created; thus, sometimes the end of the Kali-yuga marks the end of the world.[65]

Evola, in particular, has been highly influential on some past and contemporary fascist and reactionary movements. Like many fascists today, who see the three largest Abrahamic faiths (Judaism, Christianity, Islam) as causing weakness by valorizing the losers of society (often because these fascists see all three religions as poisoned by their origins in Judaism or reject religion as weakness under the influence of Nietzsche's philosophy), Evola excluded the Abrahamic faiths as potential sources of truth, preferring Hinduism and occult traditions.

In addition to his cyclic theory of history, Evola's thought was intensely racist, misogynistic, and antisemitic. Evola's racial hierarchy was borrowed from Helena Blavatsky (1831–1891), founder of the Theosophical Society; according to Blavatsky's "Polar Origin Myth,"[66] Aryans were descendants of an ancient "Atlantean" people (people of the mythical "lost island of Atlantis").[67] (This racial theory, unlike the Nazis' belief that the Aryans may have originated in northern India, which has some basis in fact, is simply myth and pseudoscience.) Evola believed there had been a takeover by a decadent, darker, and feminine southern "lunar" world, and he posited the need for a return to a northern, whiter, and masculine "solar" civilization.[68] Evola excluded Jews from this "solar civilization." Following Guénon before him, Evola cast Jews as obsessed with a monetary, "counting," and scientific view of the world that was shallow and a rejection of the allegedly deep spiritual intuition of Aryan culture. Evola wrote that "the Jewish spirit destroys everything through rationalism and calculation, leading to a world consisting of machines, things, and money instead of persons, traditions, and fatherlands."[69]

After the war, Evola urged withdrawal from modernity to wait for a more appropriate time for the social renewal of Tradition. His postwar theory took the formulation of "riding the tiger," a phrase that for Evola suggests two dimensions (which seem to me to mirror the two dimensions of catastrophic messianism as expressed by Fromm, who was critiquing fascist ideology): one a more passive form of waiting through surviving and enduring modernity, knowing that a better time cannot be achieved in one's life but keeping Tradition alive in one's private realm, and one a more active and destructive form, a strategic retreat anticipating an opportunity to accelerate the destruction of modernity. The idea of "riding the tiger" is rooted both in pessimism about historical progress and a rejection of modernity as soulless and meaningless.

Evola's fascism influenced a related fascist tendency, esoteric Hitlerism. Evola sided with the Nazis in World War II and was more welcomed by Nazi Germany than Mussolini's Italy, but his writings do not focus so much on the myth of Hitler himself. The persistence of a religion of worship around Hitler after World War II was heavily due to the popularizing efforts of "Hitler's priestess"[70] Savitri Devi. Devi—a Greek convert to Hinduism, born Maximiani Portas—moved to India in the 1930s, where she promoted Hindu nationalism and distributed fascist propaganda. After the war, she traveled to Germany to promote esoteric Hitlerism and to try to convince Germans that Hitler was alive and coming back, and she was eventually imprisoned for her illegal propagandizing. Devi's promotion of a Hitler cult was highly influential in helping Nazi ideology reorient and survive after World War II. Her postwar books such as *Kali-Yuga* and *The Lightning and the Sun* argued that Hitler was Kalki, the coming avatar of Vishnu who would reset history as predicted by the Hindu cycle.

According to Devi, the nature of reality and time is *violence*, and history is moved by certain elite figures. She argued that there are three kinds of great men, who relate themselves to the violence of time in different ways: (1) amoral, selfish tyrants, known as "Men in Time"; (2) religious mystics, known as "Men Above Time"; and (3) those who destroy in order to create, known as "Men Against Time." Men in Time destroy structures that stand in the way of transformation, preparing the way for Men Against Time, who remake history and society. Men Above Time keep Tradition alive among a select group, while it declines in society at large. Devi classified Hitler as a Man Against Time[71] who would restore a proper caste hierarchy throughout the world.[72] Applying Devi's schema to contemporary politics, fascists would be likely to see Trump as a Man in Time. "Like a blind force of destructive Nature," the Man in Time "has no ideology. Or rather, his ideology is himself," Devi writes.[73]

Following Devi, other fascists expanded esoteric Hitlerism and continued to defend the theory that Hitler was Kalki; these included the Chilean Nazi occultist Miguel Serrano in the 1970s,[74] whose sci-fi pantheon envisioned the white race as descendants of gods from another universe, who live in a realm illumined by a "Black Sun"[75] (symbolized by the sonnenrad, a Nazi symbol often substituted for the swastika). Today, related conspiracy theories and mythic, cultic discourse about UFOs, the archeological powers of "ancient aliens," secret Antarctic bases, the lost civilization of Atlantis, and so on continue to intersect with, and be infiltrated by, Nazi and racist theories that continue the legacies of Evola, Devi, and Serrano.

A resurgence of this mythology became particularly visible in the United States leading up to and following the 2016 presidential election, when a semi-satirical fascist religion known as the "cult of kek" formed to celebrate the rise of Trump and to "meme" him into power, with some using the slogan "Hail Kek," sharing memes of Pepe the frog, and waving a "Kekistani" flag that was an unabashed knock-off of a German war flag. Some called Trump the "God-Emperor" or presented Trump as Kalki, who has come at last to end the Kali-yuga. The cult of kek prized chaos and bullying humor as having the power to transform and remake society—the word "kek" was used both to refer to a made-up ancient Egyptian god of chaos and to denote laughter online. Memes change rapidly, but fascism continues to employ symbols and bullying humor in the service of obscurantist, anti-rational defense of hierarchy and its palingenetic, apocalyptic political program.

Confronting Catastrophic Messianism as a Political Task

To sum up, the problem with the accelerationist or fascist project of "destroying the world to save it" is not that it contains a utopian vision, i.e., a dream of a future that is dramatically otherwise. In fact, in many ways, fascism resigns pessimistically to injustice and then embraces it and becomes an agent of unjust action in the world. As we have seen, the belief that "might makes right" and that force is simply the natural order of the world is a significant part of the fascist belief system.

The assumption that fascism's destructive potential is caused by a desire for a world that is dramatically different has roots in the Cold War rhetoric that saw fascism and communism as equally fueled by dreams of transformation. Capitalist ideology pessimistically defends the status quo by classifying all desires for radical change, including the dream of the oppressed for liberation, as only capable of producing new forms of oppression. As we will see in

Chapter 4, contentment with the status quo is often seen as the alternative to "extremes" on both sides, which ignores the ways in which racist extremism is supported by mainstream structures.

Fascist accelerationism is "actively," politically nihilistic, in the sense of Albert Camus's definition in his perennial critique of political nihilism in *The Rebel: An Essay on Man in Revolt*, where he defines it as the pure "desire to despair and negate."[76] The void that fascism attempts to fill, discussed in Chapter 1, only *widens* as the idol of fascism is used to fill it. First, this occurs because fascism rejects morality and valorizes violence, power as opposed to reason, and mere strength to survive through brutality, and none of these successfully answer life's existential questions. Second, the void widens because violence emerges not only in defense of this fragile (idolatrous) sense of identity, but the idol itself also contains a commitment to an active nihilism of destruction and remaking. This violence disconnects the individual from their own humanity and that of others.

Because accelerationism's flaw is not its "extremism" but its nihilism, accelerationism cannot be overcome by hewing to the political center. Instead, the dehumanizing and idolatrous impulse to destroy must be confronted for what it is: an attempt to fill a void through the destruction of what is. Countering accelerationism thus requires rethinking what we believe about change, both individual and societal, and challenging eliminationism and destructiveness (including those of mainstream policies and institutions) with a revolutionary politics grounded in faith in human potential.

Notes

1 See, for example, Jade Parker, "Acceleration in America: Threat Perceptions," *GNET*, February 4, 2020, https://gnet-research.org/2020/02/04/accelerationism-in-america-threat-perceptions/; Brian Hughes and Cynthia Miller-Idriss, "Uniting for Total Collapse: The January 6 Boost to Accelerationism," *The Combating Terrorism Center at West Point*, April/May 2021, https://ctc.usma.edu/uniting-for-total-collapse-the-january-6-boost-to-accelerationism/; Matthew Kriner on Behalf of ARC Steering Committee, "An Introduction to Militant Accelerationism," *Accelerationism Research Consortium*, May 31, 2023, https://www.accresearch.org/shortanalysis/an-introduction-to-militant-accelerationism; Matthew Kriner, Meghan Conroy, and Yasmine Ashwal, "Understanding Accelerationist Narratives: 'There is No Political Solution,'" *GNET*, September 2, 2021, https://gnet-research.org/2021/09/02/understanding-accelerationist-narratives-there-is-no-political-solution/.
2 *Yeah Nah Pasaran.* "H.E. Upchurch on IronMarch, O9A, and International Fascist Terrorism." March 4, 2021, https://www.3cr.org.au/yeahnahpasaran/episode-202103041630/he-upchurch-iron-march.
3 BBC Russian Service, "How a Moscow Man from the Uzbek Family Started the World's Biggest Neo-Nazi Forum," *Meduza*, February 4, 2020, https://meduza.io/en/feature/2020/02/04/how-a-moscow-man-from-an-uzbek-family-started-the-world-s-biggest-neo-nazi-forum.
4 Nick Land, "Hyper-Racism," Affirmative Right (Formerly on Land's Blog Outside In), October 14, 2014, https://affirmativeright.blogspot.com/2014/10/hyper-racism.html.

5 Nick Land, "Occult Xenosystems," *Outside In: Involvements with Reality*, October 11, 2014, https://web.archive.org/web/20180106084441/http://www.xenosystems.net/occult-xenosystems/.

6 Neiwert, *Red Pill, Blue Pill*, vii.

7 Neiwert, *Red Pill, Blue Pill*, vii.

8 Graham Macklin, "'Praise the Saints': The Cumulative Momentum of Transnational Extreme-Right Terrorism," in *A Transnational History of Right-Wing Terrorism: Political Violence and the Far Right in Eastern and Western Europe Since 1900*, eds. Johannes Dafinger and Moritz Florin (London: Routledge, 2022), 215–40, 225.

9 *Siege*, 30.

10 *Siege*, 30.

11 Next Leap, 7.

12 Sean Musgrave, "How White Nationalists Fooled the Media about the Florida Shooter," *Politico*, February 16, 2018, https://www.politico.com/story/2018/02/16/florida-shooting-white-nationalists-415672.

13 I am borrowing this formulation of the mindset from Aaron Winter, who has written on the faulty assumption that Nazis and Islamists are in league. (Aaron Winter, 'My Enemies Must Be Friends: The American Extreme Right, Conspiracy Theory, Islam and the Middle East', *Conspiracy Theories in the Middle East and the United States*, eds, M. Reinkowski and M. Butter (Berlin: de Gruyter, 2014)).

14 Jade Parker, "Acceleration in America: Threat Perceptions," *GNET*, February 4, 2020, https://gnet-research.org/2020/02/04/accelerationism-in-america-threat-perceptions/.

15 Brian Hughes and Cynthia Miller-Idriss, "Uniting for Total Collapse: The January 6 Boost to Accelerationism," *The Combating Terrorism Center at West Point*, April/May 2021, https://ctc.usma.edu/uniting-for-total-collapse-the-january-6-boost-to-accelerationism/.

16 Hughes and Miller-Idriss, "Uniting for Total Collapse: The January 6 Boost to Accelerationism"[authors' italics].

17 NPR [@NPR]: "It appears that the Highland Park shooting suspect has no ideological or political bent. Yet extremism researchers say these acts may actually be part of a troubling new trend. One that involves dark subcultures that glorify violence and foster nihilism. https://t.co/PZR5iTjGqp," *Twitter*, July 9, 2022, https://twitter.com/NPR/status/1544819801767419905.

18 Abbie Richards, "Examining White Supremacist and Militant Accelerationist Trends on TikTok" *GNet*, July 18, 2022, https://gnet-research.org/2022/07/18/examining-white-supremacist-and-militant-accelerationism-trends-on-tiktok/.

19 Daveed Gartenstein-Ross, Andrew Zammit, Emelie Chace-Donahue, and Madison Urban, "Composite Violent Extremism: Conceptualizing Attackers Who Increasingly Challenge Traditional Categories of Terrorism." *Studies in Conflict and Terrorism* (2023): 1–27.

20 Interview.

21 *Next Leap*, 29.

22 *Next leap*, 22–3.

23 Kevin Borgeson and Robin Valeri, "Faces of Hate," *Journal of Applied Sociology* 21, no. 2, 99–111.

24 12 Rules for What?, *Post-Internet Far Right: Fascism in the Age of the Internet* (London: Dog Section Press, 2021).

25 Rachelle Hampton, "The Black Feminists Who Saw the Alt-Right Threat Coming," *Slate*, April 23, 2019, https://slate.com/technology/2019/04/black-feminists-alt-right-twitter-gamergate.html.

26 12 Rules for What?, *Post-Internet Far Right*, 84.

27 12 Rules for What?, *Post-Internet Far Right*, 85.

28 Roger Griffin, "From Slime Mould to Rhizome: An Introduction to the Groupuscular Right," *Patterns of Prejudice* 37, no. 1 (2003): 27–50, 28.

29 Griffin, "From Slime Mould to Rhizome: An Introduction to the Groupuscular Right," 28.

30 Griffin, "From Slime Mould to Rhizome: An Introduction to the Groupuscular Right," 34.

31 Griffin, "From Slime Mould to Rhizome: An Introduction to the Groupuscular Right," 37.

32 Bratich, *On Microfascism*, 101.

33 Jack Z. Bratich, *On Microfascism: Gender, War, and Death* (Brooklyn: Common Notions, 2022).

34 Ariel Koch, "The ONA Network and the Transnationalization of Neo-Nazi Satanism" in *Studies in Conflict and Terrorism* 2022: 1–28; Nick Lowles, "Order of Nine Angles," *Hope Not Hate*, February 16, 2019, https://hopenothate.org.uk/2019/02/16/state-of-hate-2019-order-of-nine-angles/.

35 Koch, "The ONA Network and the Transnationalization of Neo-Nazi Satanism," 9.

36 Lowles.

37 Lowles.

38 Federico Finchelstein, *A Brief History of Fascist Lies* (Oakland: University of California Press, 2020), 56.

39 Adorno, "Antisemitism and Fascist Propaganda," in *The Stars Down to Earth,* 221.

40 Adorno, "Antisemitism and Fascist Propaganda," in *The Stars Down to Earth,* 229–30.

41 Martin Luther King, Jr., "Letter from Birmingham Jail." August 5, 2021, https://letterfromjail.com/.

42 Erich Fromm, *The Sane Society* (New York: Henry Holt and Company, 1955), 239.

43 Gustav Landauer, "A Free Workers' Council," 219, 218–21. *Revolution and Other Writings: A Political Reader*. Ed. and Trans. Gabriel Kuhn (Pontypool: PM Press, 2010).

44 Fromm, Anatomy of Human Destructiveness, 485.

45 Leon Trotsky, "Fascism: What It Is and How to Fight It." May 31, 2021, https://www.marxists.org/archive/trotsky/works/1944/1944-fas.htm.

46 *Prophets of Deceit*, 19.

47 *Prophets of Deceit*, 98.

48 *Prophets of Deceit*, 161.

49 *Prophets of Deceit*, 162.

50 Interview.

51 Slavros, *Next Leap*, 86.

52 Claudia Leeb, *The Politics of Repressed Guilt: The Tragedy of Austrian Silence* (Edinburgh: Edinburgh University Press, 2019) 75, 90.

53 Leeb, 218–223.

54 Frederick Douglass, *On Slavery and Civil War: Selections from His Writings* (Mineola: Dover, 2003), 32.

55 David Neiwert (@David Neiwert), "As I Was Saying." August 15, 2020, https://twitter.com/DavidNeiwert/status/1294729071163711490.

56 Neiwert, *The Eliminationists*, 11.

57 Lowenthal, 98.

58 Lowenthal, 98.

59 "Cultural Marxism" is an antisemitic conspiracy theory in circulation on the far-right, according to which the (Jewish) Frankfurt School engineered political

correctness and created a creeping Marxism in mainstream institutions (Braune, "Who's Afraid of the Frankfurt School?").
60 Lowenthal, 136.
61 Griffin, *The Nature of Fascism*, 26.
62 Burley, *Fascism Today*, 48-9.
63 Griffin, *The Nature of Fascism*, 39.
64 Luis Gonzalez-Reimann, "The Yugas: Their Importance in India and their Use by Western Intellectuals and Esoteric and New Age Writers," *Religion Compass* (2014), 357–70.
65 Gonzalez-Reimann.
66 Nicholas Goodrick-Clarke, *Black Sun: Aryan Cults, Esoteric Nazism, and the Politics of Identity*, 59.
67 Goodrick-Clarke, *Black Sun*, 80.
68 *Black Sun*, 59.
69 *Black Sun*, 65.
70 Nelson Goodrick-Clarke, *Hitler's Priestess: Savitri Devi, The Hindu-Aryan Myth, and Neo-Nazism* (New York University Press, 1998).
71 Goodrick-Clark, *Black Sun*, 97.
72 Goodrick-Clark, *Black Sun*, 97.
73 Savitri Devi, *The Lightning and the Sun*, Chapter 3, May 19, 2021, http://savitridevi.org/lightning-03.html.
74 Goodrick-Clark, *Black Sun*, 173.
75 Goodrick-Clark, *Black Sun*, 180.
76 Albert Camus, *The Rebel: An Essay on Man in Revolt*. Trans. Anthony Bower (New York: Alfred A. Knopf, 1984), 57.

Bibliography

12 Rules for What? *Post-Internet Far Right: Fascism in the Age of the Internet*. London: Dog Section Press, 2021.
Adorno, Theodor. "Antisemitism and Fascist Propaganda." In Stephen Cook, Ed. and Trans., *The Stars Down to Earth* (218–232). London: Routledge, 1994.
BBC Russian Service. "How a Moscow Man from the Uzbek Family Started the World's Biggest Neo-Nazi Forum." *Meduza*, February 4, 2020. https://meduza.io/en/feature/2020/02/04/how-a-moscow-man-from-an-uzbek-family-started-the-world-s-biggest-neo-nazi-forum.
Belew, Kathleen. *Bring the War Home: The White Power Movement and Paramilitary America*. Cambridge, MA: Harvard University Press, 2018.
Borgeson, Kevin and Robin Valeri. "Faces of Hate." *Journal of Applied Sociology* 21, no. 2 (2004): 99–111.
Braune, Joan. "Who's Afraid of the Frankfurt School? Cultural Marxism as an Antisemitic Conspiracy Theory." *Journal of Social Justice* (2019): 1–25.
Burley, Shane. *Fascism Today: What It Is and How to End It*. Chico: AK Press, 2017.
Camus, Albert. *The Rebel: An Essay on Man in Revolt*. Trans. Anthony Bower. New York: Alfred A. Knopf, 1984.
Devi, Savitri. The Lighting and the Sun. Chapter 3, May 19, 2021. http://savitridevi.org/lightning-03.html.
Douglass, Frederick. *On Slavery and Civil War: Selections from His Writings*. Mineola: Dover, 2003.
Evola, Julius. *Ride the Tiger: Survival Manual for Aristocrats of the Soul*. Trans. Jocelyn Goodwin and Constance Fontana. Rochester: Inner Traditions, 2003.

Finchelstein, Federico. *A Brief History of Fascist Lies*. Oakland: University of California Press, 2020.

Fromm, Erich. *The Anatomy of Human Destructiveness*. Greenwich: Fawcett Publications, 1973.

Gartenstein-Ross, Daveed, Andrew Zammit, Emelie Chace-Donahue and Madison Urban. "Composite Violent Extremism: Conceptualizing Attackers Who Increasingly Challenge Traditional Categories of Terrorism." *Studies in Conflict and Terrorism* (2023): 1–27.

Gonzalez-Reimann, Luis. "The Yugas: Their Importance in India and their Use by Western Intellectuals and Esoteric and New Age Writers." *Religion Compass* 8, no. 12 (2014): 357–70.

Goodrick-Clarke, Nelson. *Black Sun: Aryan Cults, Esoteric Nazism, and the Politics of Identity*. New York: New York University Press, 2002.

Goodrick-Clarke, Nelson. *Hitler's Priestess: Savitri Devi, The Hindu-Aryan Myth, and Neo-Nazism*. New York: New York University Press, 1998.

Griffin, Roger. "From Slime Mould to Rhizome: An Introduction to the Groupuscular Right." *Patterns of Prejudice* 37, no. 1 (2003): 27–50.

Griffin, Roger. *The Nature of Fascism*. London: Routledge: 1993.

Griffin, Roger. "Shattering Crystals: The Role of 'Dream Time' in Extreme Right-Wing Political Violence." *Terrorism and Political Violence* 15 (2003): 57–95.

Hampton, Rachelle. "The Black Feminists Who Saw the Alt-Right Threat Coming," *Slate*, April 23, 2019. https://slate.com/technology/2019/04/black-feminists-alt-right-twitter-gamergate.html.

Hughes, Brian and Cynthia Miller-Idriss. "Uniting for Total Collapse: The January 6 Boost to Accelerationism." *The Combating Terrorism Center at West Point*, April/May 2021. https://ctc.usma.edu/uniting-for-total-collapse-the-january-6-boost-to-accelerationism/.

King, Jr., Martin Luther. "Letter from Birmingham Jail." August 5, 2021. https://letterfromjail.com/.

Koch, Ariel. "The ONA Network and the Transnationalization of Neo-Nazi Satanism." *Studies in Conflict and Terrorism* (2022): 1–28.

KOMO News. *Seattle is Dying*. March 19, 2019. https://www.youtube.com/watch?v=bpAi70WWBlw&t=2s.

Kriner, Matthew, on Behalf of ARC Steering Committee. "An Introduction to Militant Accelerationism." *Accelerationism Research Consortium*, May 31, 2023. https://www.accresearch.org/shortanalysis/an-introduction-to-militant-accelerationism.

Kriner, Matthew, Meghan Conroy, and Yasmine Ashwal, "Understanding Accelerationist Narratives: 'There is No Political Solution,' Global Network on Extremism and Technology." September 2, 2021. https://gnet-research.org/2021/09/02/understanding-accelerationist-narratives-there-is-no-political-solution/.

Land, Nick. "Hyper-Racism." *Affirmative Right*, October 14, 2014. https://affirmativeright.blogspot.com/2014/10/hyper-racism.html.

Land, Nick. "Occult Xenosystems." *Outside In: Involvements with Reality*, October 11, 2014. https://web.archive.org/web/20180106084441/http://www.xenosystems.net/occult-xenosystems/.

Landauer, Gustav. "A Free Workers' Council.". In Gabriel Kuhn, Ed. and Trans., *Revolution and Other Writings: A Political Reader* (218–21). Pontypool: PM Press, 2010.

Leeb, Claudia. *The Politics of Repressed Guilt: The Tragedy of Austrian Silence*. Edinburgh: Edinburgh University Press, 2019.

Lifton, Robert Jay. *Destroying the World to Save It: Aum Shinrikyo, Apocalyptic Violence, and the New Terrorism*. New York: Henry Holt and Company, 2000.

Lowenthal, Leo. *False Prophets: Studies on Authoritarianism*. New Brunswick: Transaction Publishers, 2016.

Lowles, Nick. "Order of Nine Angles." *Hope Not Hate*, February 16, 2019. https://hopenothate.org.uk/2019/02/16/state-of-hate-2019-order-of-nine-angles/.

Macklin, Graham. "'Praise the Saints': The Cumulative Momentum of Transnational Extreme-Right Terrorism." In Johannes Dafinger and Moritz Florin, Eds., *A Transnational History of Right-Wing Terrorism: Political Violence and the Far Right in Eastern and Western Europe Since 1900* (215–40). London: Routledge, 2022.

Musgrave, Sean. "How White Nationalists Fooled the Media about the Florida Shooter." *Politico*, February 16, 2018. https://www.politico.com/story/2018/02/16/florida-shooting-white-nationalists-415672.

Neiwert, David. *The Eliminationists: How Hate Talk Radicalized the American Right*. New York: Routledge, 2016.

Neiwert, David. *Red Pill, Blue Pill: How to Counteract the Conspiracy Theories that are Killing Us*. Lanham, MD: Prometheus Books, 2020.

NPR [@NPR]: "It Appears that the Highland Park Shooting Suspect Has No Ideological or Political Bent. "Yet Extremism Researchers Say These Acts May Actually Be Part of a Troubling New Trend. One that Involves Dark Subcultures that Glorify Violence and Foster Nihilism. https://t.co/PZR5iTjGqp." *Twitter*, July 9, 2022. https://twitter.com/NPR/status/1544819801767419905.

Parker, Jade. "Acceleration in America: Threat Perceptions." *GNET*, February 4, 2020. https://gnet-research.org/2020/02/04/accelerationism-in-america-threat-perceptions/.

Richards, Abbie. "Examining White Supremacist and Militant Accelerationist Trends on TikTok." *GNet*, July 18, 2022. https://gnet-research.org/2022/07/18/examining-white-supremacist-and-militant-accelerationism-trends-on-tiktok/.

Slavros, Alexander. "Next Leap: An IronMarch Anthology." *IronMarch*, 2018.

Slavros, Alexander and Charles Chapel. "A Squire's Trial." *IronMarch*, 2015.

Trotsky, Leon. *Fascism: What It Is and How to Fight It*. https://www.marxists.org/archive/trotsky/works/1944/1944-fas.htm.

Winter, Aaron. "My Enemies Must Be Friends: The American Extreme Right, Conspiracy Theory, Islam and the Middle East." In M. Reinkowski and M. Butter, Eds., *Conspiracy Theories in the Middle East and the United States* (35–58). Berlin: de Gruyter, 2014.

Yeah Nah Pasaran. "H.E. Upchurch on IronMarch, O9A, and International Fascist Terrorism." March 4, 2021. https://www.3cr.org.au/yeahnahpasaran/episode-202103041630/he-upchurch-iron-march.

3

STEVE BANNON'S KALI-YUGA

The desires and narratives that attract individuals to accelerationism or catastrophic messianism, as discussed in Chapter 2, do not always manifest in seemingly bizarre or plainly illegal action. "Accelerationism" under its broader definition—a strategy based on the belief that the best or only way to transform society is to first cause chaos, violence, and social collapse, because history "resets" itself through destruction—is not only a fringe criminal phenomenon. Accelerationism also emanates from the halls of power. In this chapter, I turn to Steve Bannon, a far-right political schemer and "outsider as insider,"[1] whose politics seek the destructive remaking of the world.

Bannon rose to power through far-right ranks. Throughout his time in Trump's circles, Bannon was both an insider and an outsider,[2] at the president's side influencing the policies of the most powerful government on the earth yet still shaping and flaunting an identity as a "peasant" to the "Washington elites." ("We're the peasants with pitchforks storming the lord's manor."[3]) His despise of past leaders of the establishment seemed mutual, yet as he ascended, he could be found meeting with such establishment figures as Henry Kissinger at one moment or promoting Erik Prince of military contractor Blackwater for Senate at the next. Bannon's "populist" rhetoric should not deceive us—Bannon's professed passion for "the little guy"[4] stands in tension with his profoundly hierarchical elitism: his belief that only the few are destined to know and to rule.

As we shall see, Bannon has long engaged with the thought of the Traditionalist School discussed in Chapter 2 (Julius Evola, René Guénon, etc.), first as a young man in the Navy and later in the '90s. Bannon is fascinated by a mythic, cyclical vision of history requiring the acceleration of the destruction of the present. As I argued in Chapter 2, destructiveness

DOI: 10.4324/9781003031604-4

arising from the view that the present is wholly rotten can give an illusory appearance of being truly revolutionary due to its anger, militancy, and sense of urgency, but, in fact, it serves reactionary and authoritarian purposes. A truly revolutionary politics builds on the potential (even in the form of unseen contradictions) of the present and would need to challenge Bannon's reactionary vision.

Steve Bannon: Outsider as Insider

As Donald Trump's chief campaign strategist and later advisor in the White House, Steve Bannon was widely regarded as the "brains" behind the early Trump administration and presumed by some to be the source of many White House decisions. Bannon is a former Navy officer, Pentagon staffer, Goldman Sachs investment banker, tech-world millionaire, filmmaker, Tea Party agitator, and former head of far-right website *Breitbart*. He helped to stir a "populist" upsurge in the Republican Party, promoting the Tea Party and Sarah Palin, before linking to the Trump campaign as the lead campaign advisor and then serving in the White House as an advisor in the first eight months of the Trump administration. Through his podcast, *War Room Pandemic*, he organized to cast doubt on the legitimacy of the 2020 presidential election. That year he faced federal criminal charges for allegedly grifting from a "Build the Wall" fundraiser event on the border but was pardoned by Trump the day before Trump's departure from office. Bannon remained active, building and shaping a global far-right network, pushing far-right Republican rank and file to run for low-level political positions, including those involving vote counting and working with Chinese billionaire Guo Wengui to organize a diaspora of Chinese dissidents into a confrontational reactionary force. In 2022, he faced additional charges at the state level concerning the "Build the Wall" money, and he was convicted in separate criminal proceedings for his refusal to testify or turn over documents to the U.S. congressional committee investigating the January 6 incursion into the U.S. Capitol. (He was sentenced to four months in prison and a fine and is appealing the decision.)

During his time in the Trump administration, Bannon was in and out of favor and constantly at odds with the inner circle of Trump relatives (Ivanka and Jared, whom Bannon allegedly called a "globalist" and a "cuck"[5]). Bannon stayed behind the scenes but desired power. He propitiated Trump, positioning himself as a treasured advisor, but also called himself "President Bannon"[6] and talked of a 2020 presidential run.[7] In the early administration, Bannon was given a controversial position on the National Security Council but was removed preceding Trump's bombing of Syria, presumably over disagreement on the intervention. Shortly following the August 2017 "Unite the Right" rally in Charlottesville, Virginia (which Trump said had "very fine people" on both sides), Bannon and Sebastian Gorka, a member of the "Bannon wing," left the administration. The exits of Bannon and Gorka left Stephen Miller behind as the clearest remaining member of the Bannon wing in the Trump administration ("the last man behind enemy lines," as Bannon put it[8]), although technically other Bannon associates remained in less significant roles, such as the young Julia Hahn, a former *Breitbart* reporter.

Upon leaving the Trump administration, Bannon came out swinging. Bannon began describing himself as "unleashed," and "going barbarian," and "off the chain" "for Trump." In fall 2017, Bannon seemed poised to take the Republican Party by storm, as he selected and promoted candidates. However, Bannon's and Trump's political program suffered significant defeats at the polls that November, including the defeat of gubernatorial candidate Ed Gillespie in Bannon's home state of Virginia; Gillespie had taken a hard line on immigration and received warm support from Bannon's camp. This was followed by the defeat of far-right Christian fundamentalist and accused pedophile, Roy Moore, in Alabama, for whom Bannon had campaigned vociferously, even bringing Britain's Nigel Farage to Alabama to campaign for Moore. This was to be a test case that Bannon hoped would prove to Trump the necessity of moving further right and supporting "populist economic nationalism," but Bannon's candidate lost the election. Bannon suffered a dramatic break from Trump in January 2018, after Michael Wolff's exposé *Fire and Fury: Inside the Trump White House* quoted Bannon labeling a meeting between Trump officials and Russians "treasonous."

In 2020 Bannon began to focus heavily on China. With the support of Chinese billionaire Guo Wengui,[9] Bannon also began his six-day-a-week podcast *War Room Pandemic*. Wengui and Bannon announced plans for a "New Federal State of China" and sealed their preferred leadership and principles of government with a ritualistic blood oath on a boat, accompanied by the flag they had designed for their new Chinese state.[10] Bannon also collaborated with the far-right *Epoch Times* newspaper, which is closely connected to the intensely anticommunist and pro-Trump Chinese Falun Gong cult, and produced a docudrama for a Falun Gong television platform.[11]

Bannon continued building a global far-right network, including meeting with far-right leaders like Aleksandr Dugin and Olahvo de Carvahlo,[12] and backing a takeover of the international media Voice of America news network by Michael Pack, who "cites Steve Bannon as his mentor."[13] Through his podcast, Bannon sought to mobilize far-right Republican outsiders to take over the party and the elections process at the grassroots, by obtaining lower-level positions like precinct committee officer positions and getting involved in vote counting and election watching.[14] As of this writing, Bannon has been held in contempt of court and is facing possible charges for refusing to comply with a subpoena to testify and present documents to the congressional committee investigating the January 6 incursion at the Capitol.

Destruction and Deconstruction

Although Bannon is more of a propaganda artist and political manipulator than a philosopher, he has a distinctive vision of how history operates. Bannon's vision is apocalyptic, in the sense discussed in Chapter 2, of "destroying the world to save it." Bannon no doubt hoped for the era of the Trump presidency to be conflictual and disordered. "Chaos was Steve's strategy," said Trump staffer Katie Walsh.[15] Almost immediately, Bannon made sure the "Muslim ban" was released on a Friday to stir protests—"so the snowflakes would show up at the airports and riot."[16]

Bannon played a significant role in shaping the ideology of Trumpism. He helped shape for Trump "a nationalist, divisive campaign in which issues of race, immigration, culture, and identity were put front and center."[17] He "was trying to build an intellectual basis for Trumpism, or what might more accurately be described as an American nationalist-Traditionalism."[18] And although he was wary of Trump's mercurial personality and easily wounded pride, and frequently praised him obsequiously, Bannon was also always aware of his own ideological role, pompously opining about his "destiny" and "dharma."[19] "I am the leader of the national-populist movement,"[20] he told Michael Wolff.

The power that Bannon saw in Trump lay in his destructive potential, his ability to shake up social order and perhaps, with Evola and the Traditionalists, to speed the end of the Kali-yuga. When Bannon told *Vanity Fair* in the lead-up to taking charge of the campaign that Trump was a "blunt instrument for us,"[21] perhaps he meant not that Trump would be difficult to use but that Trump would work as intended: the goal was not fine surgery but the release of sudden, uncontrolled destructive energy. In esoteric Hitlerist Savitri Devi's terms, Trump would be considered a "Man in Time," and perhaps Bannon himself theorized Trump in these terms, drawing on Devi. Benjamin Teitelbaum's book *War for Eternity* explores Bannon's and white nationalists' ties to Traditionalism. (Note: Teitelbaum has received scrutiny for an article on the need for an "immoral anthropology," including friendships with fascists as a research method or acceptable outcome of research.[22]) According to Teitelbaum, Bannon seemed to identify Trump as a "Man in Time" and Bannon himself as a "Man Against Time."[23] As a Man in Time, Trump's role would be that of an amoral destroyer; Bannon's role as a "Man Against Time" would position him as a conscious restorer of past harmony and a director of the historical cycle.

Bannon has since sought to exacerbate controversy over the 2020 election, which Bannon stoked on his podcast calling for a "knife fight"[24] over ballot counting in the lead-up to the election. His task in the Trump administration was, as Bannon put it (in a definitive speech at the Conservative Political Action Conference, laying out his approach early in the Trump administration), in part a project of "deconstruction," the "deconstruction of the administrative state." In the same vein is Bannon's sardonic self-description as a "Leninist"—"Lenin wanted to destroy the state, and that's my goal too. I want to bring everything crashing down, and destroy all of today's establishment."[25] Reading the fiercely anticommunist Bannon (who portrays Reagan as a god-like figure) as a literal Leninist would be a mistake—rather, Bannon is an authoritarian with a mythic, destructive vision, and he is awestruck by any figure who is able to tear down massive structures, perhaps seeing in Lenin the power to mobilize the masses for destruction. (The reference to Lenin also perhaps evokes founder of the libertarian Cato Institute Murray Rothbard's foundational programmatic document *Towards a Strategy for Libertarian Social Change*, which heavily quoted Lenin on strategy and argued for the formation of a libertarian "cadre."[26])

This destructiveness manifests in an obsession with war, with Bannon even using "#war" as a slogan, naming his podcast the "war room," and nicknaming his duplex "Sparta."[27] According to the past friend of Bannon, Julia Jones, Bannon was enamored with the Hindu *Bhagavad Gita* and "used to talk a lot about dharma—he felt very strongly about dharma."[28] Jones sees Bannon's love of the *Gita*, an allegorical text that takes place in a war zone, where the god Krishna exhorts Arjuna not to flee from the battle but to fight bravely, as falling within a wider fascination Bannon has with war, describing "books all over [Steve's place] about battles and things...He talked *a lot* about Sparta—how Sparta defeated Athens, he loved the story."[29] "Steve is a strong militarist," she is quoted as saying. "He's in love with war—it's almost poetry to him."[30]

Bannon's Engagement with Traditionalism and the Fourth Turning

Bannon's appreciation for the Traditionalist School (discussed in Chapter 2) is well known and much commented upon. Bannon has cited René Guénon's *Man and His Becoming According to the Vedanta* as a "life-changing discovery."[31] He also cited Evola in a speech to a right-wing Catholic think tank and praised Milo Yiannopolous for discussing Evola in an article on the alt-right for *Breitbart*.[32] Furthermore, by Bannon's account, this fascination is long-running; already as a young man in the Navy, Bannon was reading esoteric and mystical texts, including Blavatsky, and by the early 1990s, he had contacted Jacob Needleman, a Traditionalist scholar and follower of Gurdjieff in California.[33]

Before Bannon's fascination with fascist "Traditionalist" thinkers like Evola became more publicly known, much attention was paid to Bannon's promotion of William Strauss and Neil Howe's book *The Fourth Turning: What the Cycles of History Tell Us about America's Next Rendezvous with Destiny*, which can be read as a popularization of some of the theories of the Traditionalist School. *The Fourth Turning* is one of Bannon's chief talking points, and it is not often discussed in the context of his fascination with Traditionalism, but the two are clearly connected.

Although *The Fourth Turning* does not express support for Traditionalism directly, it is based on a cyclical theory of history that it also draws partly from Hinduism and applies to politics. The authors also, if not consciously Traditionalists, draw from some overlapping sources, such as Mircea Eliade, Oswald Spengler, and Carl Jung,[34] and briefly mention the Kali-yuga.

According to Strauss and Howe, each cyclical decline begins when a generation of utopian-minded hippies (a "prophet generation") disrupts peaceful periods of stability, tradition, and economic success. The subsequent decades of decline in social order can only be reinstated by a new "hero generation," which wages a bloody conflict to restore what was lost by the utopians that preceded them. Bannon likely sees a particular role for Millennials as a hero generation, in leading a right-wing reactionary battle on a world scale, ending the Kali-yuga.

The coming Crisis, according to Strauss and Howe, might simply lead to a rebirth of the United States on a firmer footing, but it could lead to more dramatic results. In fact, Strauss and Howe state that there are four possible outcomes of the coming Crisis, including the end of humanity in an "omnicidal Armageddon, destroying everything, leaving nothing"[35] or the end of modernity: "a total war, terrible but not final" leading to "a complete collapse of science, culture, politics, and society."[36] Strauss and Howe suggest that the most likely outcome, less drastic than the first two, could be an end to the United States of America.[37] The fourth possibility suggested by Strauss and Howe is simply another rebirth of the United States, without the end of the country, modernity, or humanity.[38]

Bannon worked with *Fourth Turning* author Neil Howe on "several film projects."[39] Under Bannon's chairmanship, far-right website *Breitbart* ran *dozens* of articles drawing on Strauss and Howe's "Generational Dynamics" theories, regularly reprinting headlines from a blog devoted to applying Strauss and Howe's theories to geopolitics. Strauss and Howe's consulting firm, Life Course Associates, which is based on Strauss and Howe's theories about history and the "generations" that shape historical change, has consulted with dozens of powerful organizations and companies, including Goldman Sachs, Ford, JP Morgan, the National Rifle Association, Booz Allen, Northrop Grummon, and Raytheon.[40] Life Course Associates worked closely with the U.S. military to improve recruitment of Millennials, including writing a handbook called *Recruiting Millennials* that was distributed to 8,000 U.S. Army recruiters.[41]

Although economic and environmental crisis, rising racism and fascism, and Western imperial ambitions and ongoing global conflicts do give rise to an image of global catastrophe, Strauss and Howe are not so much assessing current risks as outlining an ontology of history. Their vision is mythic, not scientific.

According to Strauss and Howe, historical drama recurs in a cycle (or "Saeculum") of four, roughly 20–25 year intervals known as "turnings"; a full cycle is accomplished approximately every century. Strauss and Howe title these turnings "The High," "The Awakening," "The Unraveling," and "The Crisis." The last "High" was the 1950s. We are currently, by Straus and Howe's timeline, in the Crisis, their version of the Kali-yuga. According to Strauss and Howe, each Crisis ends in an *ekpyrosis*—a destruction and a rebirth—which must periodically occur in order for history to continue. At the end of each full cycle, according to Strauss and Howe, a mythical "Gray Champion" appears and leads a new generation into battle to restore what was lost. (Of course, some wonder whether Bannon thinks he is the Gray Champion.[42])

Bannon made a film about the "fourth turning" theory, *Generation Zero*, a peculiarly apocalyptic homage to the Tea Party; although ostensibly about the 2008 financial crisis, the film's core commitment is catastrophism. *Generation Zero* is structured around the Strauss-Howe four turnings theory and builds on Strauss and Howe's theory of "prophet generations" and "Awakening" periods, to blame the hippies and the spirit of the 1960s for the subprime mortgage crisis and 2008 financial collapse. The 1960s "Awakening," according to Bannon's film, failed to acknowledge natural limits to happiness and success and did not honor the wisdom of elders (or ancestors, one might say). Untamed hippie optimism gave way to economic speculation, ringing in the third turning, the "Unraveling." The hippies, with their utopian visions, entered politics, the media, entertainment, and the universities, bringing their idea of the possibility of total success and with it the certainty of collapse. Crucially, according to the film, Crises may arrive inevitably or may be instigated by a "fourth-turning leader" who will "encourage [a crisis] to happen."

Generations: Hamsters on the Wheel of Samsara

Whomever he envisions as the vanguard of the next "rendezvous with destiny," Bannon anticipates that the Millennial generation is the "hero generation" destined to fight and win the coming battles, moving history out of Crisis and back to High. In the process, he will continue to try to assemble a reactionary fighting force of youth. As Bannon's brother says, Bannon "collects people,"[43] and he seems to be particularly interested in collecting youth.

In an appearance on a podcast called *Red Scare*, which is best understood as far-right while appropriating concepts in various ways from the left, Bannon told the young hosts that Millennials specifically will be the next "greatest generation."[44] He played as well on the Millennial experience of economic loss, painting an image of Millennials circling a void: "You're just a hamster on the wheel of samsara...one or two paychecks away from oblivion."[45]

Perhaps Bannon's vision of a Millennial-generation reactionary force makes him think of some of *Breitbart*'s young employees during his tenure there. "We hire freaks," Bannon said of the young far-right news junkies, trolls, and ideologues he collected at *Breitbart*.[46] He compared *Breitbart*'s macho young reactionary climate to the "honey badger,"[47] the fearless hunter unfazed by attackers, and called *Breitbart* "fight club."[48] It was under Bannon that Milo Yiannopolous became a rising star at *Breitbart*, acting as a provocateur on campuses around the nation. (Bannon said of Milo, "Milo is an amoral nihilist. I knew right away, he's gonna be a fucking meteor."[49])

What role do fascist youth play in Bannon's coming "hero generation"? Under Bannon's chairmanship, *Breitbart* repeatedly praised the neo-fascist youth of the Identitarian Movement, the small but frightening movement of anti-immigrant reactionaries founded in France as Generation Identitaire. Bannon also referred to the "alt-right" favorably as "younger people who are anti-globalists, very nationalist, terribly anti-establishment."[50] (Some of the shifting claims of identification and disidentification with the alt-right on Bannon's part, no doubt, come from the shift toward the term "alt-right" becoming more exclusively tied to Nazis in the public's perception from the lead-up to Trump's election to after the Charlottesville hate march. However, Bannon earlier helped to promote the term and published an article on *Breitbart* by Milo Yiannopolous that helped to popularize it, including linking the alt-right to Evola's fascist Traditionalism.[51])

Signaling Affinities and Building Alliances

When Bannon or anyone else wants to argue that Bannon's political philosophy is not based on racism or antisemitism, they can easily find data to marshal in their defense. Bannon has said that Evola is "not a great guy"[52] and that Bannon does not endorse Evola's fascism.[53] Hagiographic court biographer of Bannon, Keith Koffler, marshals various friends and former friends of Bannon to assert that Bannon is not racist or antisemitic,[54] and while this is not in itself persuasive, Bannon could certainly dredge up others as needed.

It is clear that Bannon wants to be able to have it both ways: to be seen as racist by elements of the openly racist far-right and to be seen as not racist (i.e., as falsely accused and persecuted) by conservatives who are not consciously racist. It is also important to note that not all fascists and white supremacists like him, and some who were hopeful now feel let down.

Bannon is a case study in normalization of fascist ideology—*fascism as a social movement seeking power, always already connected to sources of power.* He has often signaled affinities with fascist ideologues and professed support for Traditionalist thinkers. For example (one of *many* examples), Bannon was fascinated by J.R.R. Tolkien and *The Lord of the Rings* movies and began in fall 2017 to refer to Trump's supporters as "hobbits." Did Bannon know that the Italian fascist movement in the 1970s had organized a series of "Hobbit Camps,"[55] a kind of "fascist Woodstock," based on a fascist interpretation of Tolkien's novels? Plausible deniability, but surely Bannon is likely to have known, and either way, experienced fascists, remembering the "Hobbit Camps," hear that extra edge.

They hear it when Bannon calls Martin Heidegger "my guy"[56] (the German philosopher was a Nazi, and his ideas are used as building blocks by a number of fascist thinkers today, including Aleksandr Dugin[57]); when Bannon says of Mussolini that he "was clearly loved by women...a guy's guy. He has all that virility. He also had amazing fashion sense, right, that whole thing with the uniforms. I'm fascinated by Mussolini"[58]; when Bannon praises French far-right nationalist and antisemite Charles Maurras, or the virulently racist novel *Camp of the Saints*;[59] or when Bannon calls the young women writers of Breitbart "Valkyries,"[60] fearsome figures of Norse mythology, likely a nod to Richard Wagner.

They hear it when they learn that Bannon wanted to be "the Leni Riefenstahl of the GOP,"[61] referencing the famous propaganda filmmaker for the Nazis.

They hear it when Bannon marvels over the "German industrial design" and "precision engineering" of Birkenau concentration camp, somewhat dwarfing his expression of horror, which feels somehow more *pro forma*.[62]

They hear it when he calls French president Macron a "little Rothschild's banker."[63]

They hear it when he tells a French far-right audience, "Let them call you racist. Let them call you xenophobes. Let them call you nativists. Wear it as a badge of honor."[64]

And Bannon knows that they hear it. He wiggles and disclaims and, at other times, owns it. One feels for the interviewer in the documentary *The Brink*, who, after discussing Bannon's alliance that would include Farage, Duterte, Orbán, and Modi, makes a frustrated attempt to talk to Bannon about his racist dog whistles. "I don't think it's a trivial, joking sort of thing, and you do this sort of smirk, and it's sort of uncomfortable for me, because it's serious," he says. Bannon reassures him and changes the subject with a deftness that, as always, sidesteps the issue.

But Bannon does not even really need to signal. In addition to this "signaling," there is the matter of Bannon's connections/partners, as he forges a proto-fascist international, including forging links with an important advisor to Jair Bolsonaro's administration in Brazil, Olavo de Carvahlo; meeting with Aleksandr Dugin, whose commitment to Traditionalism he praised in a speech to a right-wing Catholic think tank in 2014[65] and whom he met with in 2018[66]; building a think tank called "The Movement" allied with the Belgian People's Party, Italy's Matteo Salvini, and Marine Le Pen's National Front; and pursuing an (ultimately stymied) attempt to establish a far-right "gladiator school" in a medieval Italian monastery to educate and train young right-wing leaders. Here we see Bannon's project of developing, even to some degree choosing, future leaders, from his role in Cambridge Analytica pushing Brexit and Trump, to his role in France and promoting Marine Le Pen's even further right-wing niece Marion Le Pen, to hanging out with his handpicked future president of China.

The alliances are clear, in fact. His signaling may be less about calling new allies to his side, so much as alarming those opponents who also know how to read the signals. Through this signaling, he also intensifies the conflict that he may believe can lead to the resetting of history. In the process, he also deliberately works across the lines that liberal commentators are trained to expect. Bannon's political agenda may assist the growth of "red-brown alliances" (i.e., collaboration between "leftists" and fascists), and such alliances are helped by apocalyptic visions like Bannon's that denigrate the present as a site of degeneration from a noble past and that see substantial change as only possible through catastrophe. We need to pay attention to the outreach of figures like Bannon to the left, as seen in his professed desire to transform the Republican Party into a "workers party"[67] and to design a "*Breitbart* for the left*.*" It was Bannon, for example, who reached out to unions (usually a bastion of Democratic Party voters) as part of the 2016 Trump presidential campaign strategy. Although the more thoughtful elements of the left will not be confused, Bannon will muddy the waters as much as he can, since again, his goal is to ramp up conflict and tension for a history-resetting rendezvous.

Narrative and Myth

Fascist and far-right worldviews also fail to distinguish imagination from reality in reliable ways. The far-right lives in a world of fantasy: fantasy homelands, fantasy girlfriends, fantasy battles, fantasy religions. With present-day hate phenomena, the attraction to bizarre mythologies often overlaps with gaming. The alt-right grew out of online communities including Reddit, 4chan, and the surrounding "gamergate" misogynist controversy, in which angry young men attacked feminists for critiquing misogyny in video games. Bannon himself made money from the video game *World of Warcraft*, where he helped to engineer the sale of imaginary commodities internal to the game (e.g., a shield for one's battleship). Bannon had earlier discovered the power of angry male video gamer culture, via multiplayer video game message boards like Thottbot: "These rootless white males, had monster power," Bannon told Joshua Green of the internet spaces that preceded spaces like 4chan and reddit, identified as birthplaces of the alt-right.[68] Analogous as well was Bannon's financial investment in the bizarre "Biosphere 2" project, which created an artificial reality to test survival under conditions of climate change. Bannon has continually profited from myth, but this is more than a matter of financial self-interest; he *believes* the central myth that drives his politics. The childlike fantasy of war and Manichean battles—the forces of light contending against the forces of darkness—and the video-game mythology meld in an apocalyptic vision.

The problem is not fantasy itself nor the vision of some other world, although the apparent literalness with which some narratives are accepted does show fascism's disconnection from reality and truth. Rather, the problem is fascism's *confidence that private dreamworlds can and should be asserted and violently enforced as real.* The enforcement of these dreamworlds includes the construction of a distinction between friend and enemy and a definition of what victory entails and the battle through which it is to be obtained.

Bannon's views of truth and power are tied up with his fascination with narrative and myth. Right-wing pundit Ben Shapiro, who formerly worked under Bannon, was right to note that "Narrative truth was [Bannon's] priority rather than factual truth."[69] In Bannon's film on Ronald Reagan, Bannon presents communism as a manifestation of "the Beast": "The Beast too understood the power of myth. Entire countries could [be] moved to riot or subsist in silence, to follow or revolt, to obey or disobey."[70] Bannon's fascination with Hollywood films fits the same mold; truth and right are portrayed through narrative: "Hollywood doesn't make movies where the bad guys win," Bannon told a reporter after the election, who compared Trump's win to a Hollywood film.[71]

Bannon's two biggest political organs, Cambridge Analytica and *Breitbart*, both relied on the power of myth and narrative. Bannon's Cambridge Analytica was formed as a branch of military contractor Strategic Communication Laboratories (SCL), a counter-insurgency company contracted with the British government that had already been focused on the development of narratives to shift politics.[72] As we shall see in a moment, under Bannon's direction, Cambridge Analytica deliberately raised racist fears of loss to secure votes for Brexit and for Trump. *Breitbart News* follows a similar pattern— *Breitbart* was about generating outrage not offering analysis, engaging its audience in an "ongoing drama, with distinct story lines, heroes, and villains," with themes like "immigration, ISIS, race riots, and what we call 'the collapse of traditional values," *Breitbart* editor Alex Marlow explained.[73]

Bannon's Racism

It would appear from former Cambridge Analytica tech guru Christopher Wylie's explanation that a crucial element in Bannon's plan for America with Cambridge Analytica was not only to explore how racism could be weaponized to win elections but also to actively make people more racist. For example, white Anglo parents in one Cambridge Analytica focus group were asked whether they would mind their daughter marrying a Mexican immigrant and, if they expressed approval, were asked, "Did you feel like you had to say that?" and were given the opportunity to "change their answer."[74] Others were asked to look at a list of "ethnic names" and asked whether they would mind living in a country where "you can't pronounce anyone's name." They were asked, "Do you recall a time where people were laughing at someone who messed up an ethnic name? Do some people use political correctness to make others feel dumb?"[75] Cambridge Analytica targeted Evangelicals with the "Just World Hypothesis" (the belief that the world is fundamentally fair) and asked them whether they agreed that God is just and fair and if it followed that it was the fault of minorities if they were not succeeding.[76]

The strategy was to ramp up feelings of grievance and white victimhood, and perceptions of being "silenced" by "political correctness," and to justify imbalances in society as resulting from immutable characteristics of minorities. Wylie was disturbed to see a video of a person so "provoked" by Cambridge Analytica's methods that they were frothing in racist rage and shouting slurs in a kind of frenzy.[77] Bannon believed, according to Wylie, that white Americans needed to be "deprogrammed" from the "'conditioning' they had endured growing up in a vapid and meaningless society."[78] This would enable them to "discover themselves" and "become who they really were."[79]

Bannon's language, and his studied provocation of white American grievance, suggests again the cycle of return: a declining society bereft of meaning (in the Kali-Yuga) can return to greatness through what can hardly be described as something other than a white awakening, the return of white people to a sense of expressing an inner destiny. In other words, the provocation of white grievance marked a "return" to a past golden age, an overcoming of alienation and recuperation of lost self.

Bannon would no doubt object to this characterization of his thought with regard to race (at the very least in public). He has asserted many times that his view is "populist economic nationalism" and that populist economic nationalism does not care about race, ethnicity, religion, or sexual orientation. He has also denied being an "ethno-nationalist." He frequently insists on his podcast that he hates the Communist Party of China, not the Chinese people (especially not the "old hundred names," a populist formulation from Chinese culture he compares to the characterization of Trump voters as "deplorables").

However, Bannon's notion of a country is more than a collection of individuals and includes a notion of a unified "people." Bannon told Teitelbaum:

> I'm a huge believer that we are a country with a border and a wall, and a country that has a culture and a civilization and citizens and Americanness to it all, right? And that's a country. If that's called blood and soil, then so be it. But we're a country, we're a thing, with a people and a set of customs and traditions. We're not some idea. I hate the concept that America is an idea.[80]

Bannon certainly cares about the ethnic demographic content of the United States, above and beyond putting American citizens of all races first economically, over and against non-citizens. Racism does not have to be grounded in a biologically fixed hierarchy of races but can be grounded, for example, in beliefs that members of certain groups generally happen to be inferior or dangerous due to "cultural" factors (as in the case of what Etienne Balibar theorizes as "cultural racism"). Even Evola, though clearly a racist and fascist, critiqued biologism and based his philosophy on a "spiritualized" hierarchy of races. Racism that is spiritualized as opposed to "scientific" can be just as insidious. (For example, Richard Wolin stresses the influence of Nazi-era philosopher Martin Heidegger on the New Right, including the influence of Heidegger's "spiritualized" antisemitism and racism.[81])

Bannon's cultural racism and spiritualized hierarchy enable him to categorize himself differently to the public from self-professed white nationalists, fascists, and neo-Nazis. The white supremacist propagandist famously punched at Trump's presidential inauguration, Richard Spencer, is a "goofball" according to Bannon—"you can't get in business with goofballs like that,"[82] he told Benjamin Teitelbaum. It's not entirely clear where Bannon draws the line, however, and one can, if one is Bannon, still see in the goofballs a sincerity, an expression of dharma and destiny: "We're all fighting the same fight," Bannon told a young writer for white nationalist site American Renaissance.[83] Black former Trump staffer Omarosa Manigault Newman writes in her memoir, citing a conversation in which Bannon defended white pride:

> I had an interesting conversation with Bannon and asked him if the rumors of his being a racist were true. He said no. He explained, "The same way you are a proud African American woman, I am a proud white man. What's the difference between my pride and your pride?"[84]

Bannon is excited by rising racial tension, and even the antiracist movements he opposes play a role in his grand imaginary drama. *Racist violence* seems like a central component of the envisioned Crisis preceding the Traditionalists' return of Kalki or Strauss and Howe's hero generation. Despite his claims to be a mere "economic" nationalist, Bannon's vision of a "nation" is rooted in notions of cultural identity. Bannon has favorably cited French Nazi sympathizer Charles Maurras's distinction between a mere "legal" country and the "real" country (perhaps like Sarah Palin's "Real America"), tied together by a common cultural identity.[85] In a famous interview with Trump before Bannon signed on to his campaign, Bannon resisted Trump's support for allowing highly skilled immigrants into the country: "When two-thirds or three-quarters of the CEOs in Silicon Valley are from South Asia or from Asia, I think…a country is more than an economy. We're a civic society," Bannon said.[86] That statistic happens to be false, but more to the point, the quote suggests that Bannon is not a mere "economic nationalist" as he has claimed but that he sees American identity as threatened by ethnic and cultural change. A defense of the esoteric "real nation," and a call for young white people in particular to "become who they are" through a coming battle, characterizes Bannon's racism, which is no less real despite its intellectual veneer.

Conclusion

Bannon's vision at the very least has affinities with the fascist accelerationism discussed in Chapter 2—Bannon is in some sense "destroying the world to save it." However, studying Bannon reminds us that catastrophism is not only a fringe criminal phenomenon, but it also walks the halls of power and works behind the scenes in large global networks scheming for power and collaborating with already existing sources of political power. In the terms discussed in the previous chapter, "entryism" can serve as an accelerationist tactic. For this reason, stopping the scheming of people like Bannon cannot be accomplished by the security state or the legal system alone. Although the mainstream neoliberal state is conflicted about fascism—it sometimes views it as a security threat, and Bannon may soon again face criminal charges—the security state also knows that fascism can be invited in as the keeper of order against emancipatory social movements fighting racism and economic exploitation. If Bannon goes to prison, others will take his place; the problem of reactionary scheming, the violent imposition of mythic worldviews, and the attempt to stir violence to reset history will continue.

Antifascist organizing has sometimes been described as a "three-way fight," with the antifascist needing to oppose both fascism and mainstream capitalist politics.[87] Activist researchers engaged in the three-way fight must constantly watch and expose growing far-right networks and combat their normalization. Although Bannon seeks more polarization, this does not mean that polarization is the root of the United States' current problems and that the solution is compromise, dialogue, or bridge-building with the right. The far-right must be defeated. Defeating an enemy in order to move forward is different from a catastrophist or eliminationist political project. Some conflicts have to be fought out in order to be won—Bannon knows this, and we would be fools to pretend otherwise in the name of civility or peace.

Notes

1 I discuss this framing further and the reference to Peter Gay's book *Weimar Germany: The Outsider as Insider,* Joan Braune, "The Outsider as Insider: Steve Bannon, Fourth Turnings, and the Neofascist Threat," ed. Samir Gandesha, *Spectres of Fascism: Historical, Theoretical, and International Perspectives* (London: Pluto Press, 2020), 207–22, 207 and passim.

2 Jedediah Purdy, "The Anti-Democratic Worldview of Steve Bannon and Peter Thiel," *Politico,* November 30, 2016, https://www.politico.com/magazine/story/2016/11/donald-trump-steve-bannon-peter-thiel-214490.

3 Keith Koffler, *Bannon: Always the Rebel* (Washington, DC: Regnery Publishing, 2017), 49 (citing *New York Times*).

4 Koffler.

5 Asawin Suebsaeng, "Steve Bannon Calls Jared Kushner a 'Cuck' and 'Globalist' Behind His Back," *Daily Beast,* May 5, 2017, https://www.thedailybeast.com/steve-bannon-calls-jared-kushner-a-cuck-and-globalist-behind-his-back.

6 Wolff, *Fire and Fury,* 175.

7 Wolff.

8 Jennifer Jacobs (@JenniferJJacobs) tweet, "The Last Man," October 20, 2017, https://twitter.com/JenniferJJacobs/status/921356724459753472.

9 Rosalind S. Helderman, Josh Dawsey, et al., "How former Trump adviser Steve Bannon Joined Forces with a Chinese Billionaire who has Divided the President's Allies," *Washington Post,* September 13, 2020, https://www.washingtonpost.com/politics/steve-bannon-guo-wengui/2020/09/13/8b43cd06-e964-11ea-bc79-834454439a44_story.html.

10 Meanwhile in China, "Mr. Wengui and Steve Bannon Make a Blood Oath to Destroy China," *YouTube,* June 14, 2020, https://www.youtube.com/watch?v=sdTi5HglO4g.

11 Simon van Zylen-Wood, "MAGA-land's Favorite Newspaper," *The Atlantic,* January 31, 2021, https://www.theatlantic.com/politics/archive/2021/01/inside-the-epoch-times-a-mysterious-pro-trump-newspaper/617645/?fbclid=IwAR3MWaAgU6B0SCl8TlmYLEe36TnrttTEm5mK_w_2_ZX-eRtuoiNxpYGi4zY. This article is a good introduction, on my choice to call the Falun Gong a cult: Ben Hurley, "Me and L – Why I Left Falun Gong After Being a Devoted Believer for a Decade" Me and Li — Why I left Falun Gong after being a devoted believer for a decade | by Ben Hurley | Medium, April 20, 2021.

12 Teitelbaum, *War for Eternity,* 92ff., 164ff.

13 Rachel Maddow Show, MSNBC Trump stacks US media agency with loyalists led by Bannon acolyte (msnbc.com).

14 Isaac Arnsdorf, Doug Bock Clark, et al. "Heeding Steve Bannon's Call, Election Deniers Organize to Seize Control of the GOP—And Reshape America's Elections," *Pro Publica,* September 2, 2021, https://www.propublica.org/article/heeding-steve-bannons-call-election-deniers-organize-to-seize-control-of-the-gop-and-reshape-americas-elections.

15 Wolff, *Fire and Fury,* 64.

16 Wolff, *Fire and Fury,* 65.

17 Green, 208.

18 Green, 208.

19 *American Dharma*, directed by Errol Morris. Utopia, 2002.

20 Wolff, *Fire and Fury*, 301.

21 Koffler, 163.

22 Benjamin R. Teitelbaum, "Collaborating with the Radical Right: Scholar-Informant Solidarity and the Case for an Immoral Anthropology," *Current Anthropology* 60, no. 3 (June 2019): 413–35.

23 In Teitelbaum's book, Bannon calls Trump a "man in time" (120) and a "destroyer" (117), which as Teitelbaum is aware could possibly be a reference to Kalki, the Destroyer. Teitelbaum paints Bannon as a "man against time," a title Bannon seems to accept from Teitelbaum (124). How much all of this is an accurate depiction is, of course, an open question, but Bannon has not made a public correction of Teitelbaum's book.

24 Kyle Mantyla, "Steve Bannon Wants Conservative Christian Poll Workers 'Inside the Room for the Knife Fight,'" *Right Wing Watch*, August 16, 2022, https://www.rightwingwatch.org/post/steve-bannon-wants-conservative-christian-poll-workers-inside-the-room-for-the-knife-fight/.

25 Ronald Radosh, "Steve Bannon, Trump's Top Guy, Told Me He's a 'Leninist.'" *Daily Beast*, March 13, 2017, http://www.thedailybeast.com/articles/2016/08/22/steve-bannon-trump-s-top-guy-told-me-he-was-a-leninist.html.

26 Nancy MacLean, *Democracy in Chains: The Deep History of the Radical Right's Stealth Plan for America* (New York: Penguin, 2017), 140.

27 Koffler, 43.

28 Asawin Suebsaeng, "Steve Bannon's Long Love Affair with War," *Daily Beast*, April 11, 2017, https://www.thedailybeast.com/steve-bannons-long-love-affair-with-war.

29 Suebsaeng. "Steve Bannon's Long Love Affair with War."

30 Suebsaeng. "Steve Bannon's Long Love Affair with War."

31 Green, 206.

32 Joseph Bernstein, "Here's How Breitbart and Milo Smuggled White Nationalism into the Mainstream," *Buzzfeed*, October 5, 2017, https://www.buzzfeednews.com/article/josephbernstein/heres-how-breitbart-and-milo-smuggled-white-nationalism.

33 Teitelbaum, *War for Eternity*, 27, 33.

34 Strauss and Howe, 54.

35 Strauss and Howe, 330.

36 Strauss and Howe, 330.

37 Strauss and Howe, 330–1.

38 Strauss and Howe, 331.

39 Neil Howe, "Where Did Steve Bannon Get His Worldview? From My Book," *The Washington Post*, February 24, 2017, https://www.washingtonpost.com/entertainment/books/where-did-steve-bannon-get-his-worldview-from-my-book/2017/02/24/16937f38-f84a-11e6-9845-576c69081518_story.html.

40 Life Course Associates, "Our Clients," March 18, 2017, http://www.lifecourse.com/about/clients.html.

41 Life Course Associates, "Military," April 19, 2017, http://www.lifecourse.com/practice/military.html.

42 Adele Stan, "Insurrectionist in Chief," *New Republic*, March 10, 2021, https://newrepublic.com/article/161574/steve-bannon-capitol-riots-insurrectionist-chief.

43 Koffler, 71.

44 Red Scare Podcast, "War Room Red Scare w/ Steve Bannon," April 4, 2020, July 9, 2021, https://redscarepodcast.libsyn.com/war-room-red-scare-w-steve-bannon.

45 Red Scare Podcast.

46 Paul Fahri, "How Breitbart Has Become a Dominant Voice in Conservative Media." https://www.washingtonpost.com/lifestyle/style/how-breitbart-has-become-a-dominant-voice-in-conservative-media/2016/01/27/a705cb88-befe-11e5-9443-7074c3645405_story.html?utm_term=.8ec77a9c6896 accessed June 10, 2017.

47 Green, *Devil's Bargain*, 148.

48 Fahri, "How Breitbart has Become a Dominant Voice in Conservative Media."

49 Green, 146.

50 Matea Gold, Rosalind S. Helderman, et al., "For Trump Adviser Stephen Bannon, Fiery Populism Followed Life in Elite Circles," *Washington Post*, November 19, 2016, https://www.washingtonpost.com/politics/for-trump-adviser-stephen-bannon-fiery-populism-followed-life-in-elite-circles/2016/11/19/de91ef40-ac57-11e6-977a-1030f822fc35_story.html?utm_term=.2a79678a5532.

51 Bernstein, "Here's How Breitbart and Milo Smuggled White Nationalism into the Mainstream."

52 Koffler, 114.

53 Koffler, 113.

54 Koffler, 140–1.

55 John Last, "How 'Hobbit Camps' Rebirthed Italian Fascism," *Atlas Obscura*, October 3, 2017, https://www.atlasobscura.com/articles/hobbit-camps-fascism-italy.

56 Christoph Scheuermann, "Stephen Bannon Tries Rightwing Revolution in Europe," *Der Spiegel*, accessed May 1, 2021, https://www.spiegel.de/international/world/stephen-bannon-tries-rightwing-revolution-in-europe-a-1235297.html.

57 For more on Dugin's uptake of Heidegger, see Ronald Beiner, *Dangerous Minds: Nietzsche, Heidegger, and the Return of the Far Right* (Philadelphia: University of Pennsylvania Press, 2018); Richard Wolin, *Heidegger in Ruins: Between Philosophy and Ideology* (New Haven, CT: Yale University Press, 2022).

58 Nicholas Farrell, "'I'm Fascinated by Mussolini': Steve Bannon Talks Fascism," *The Spectator*, March 18, 2018, https://spectatorworld.com/topic/mussolini-steve-bannon/.

59 Michael Crowley, "The Man Who Wants to Unmake the West," *Politico*, March 12, 2017, https://www.politico.eu/article/the-man-who-wants-to-unmake-the-west/.

60 Peter Maas, "Birth of a Radical: White Fear in the White House: Young Bannon Disciple Julia Hahn is a Case Study in Extremism," *The Intercept*, May 7, 2017, https://theintercept.com/2017/05/07/white-fear-in-the-white-house-young-bannon-disciple-julia-hahn-is-a-case-study-in-extremism/; Green, *Devil's Bargain*, 149.

61 Matt Pearce, "Steve Bannon Found Influences in Ancient Thinkers, Reagan, and Nazi Propaganda," *Los Angeles Times*, December 9, 2016. http://www.latimes.com/nation/la-na-bannon-influences-20161209-story.html.

62 *The Brink*, directed by Alison Klayman (AliKlay Productions, RYOT films, 2019).

63 Nicholas Farrell, "Steve Bannon on 'Masturbatory' Emmanuel Macron, Elites, and Old Etonians," *The Spectator World*, June 7, 2018, https://spectatorworld.com/topic/steve-bannon-rome/.

64 Mary Papenfuss, "Steve Bannon: 'Let Them Call You Racist; Wear It As a Badge of Honor," *Huffpost*, March 10, 2018, https://www.huffpost.com/entry/bannon-far-right-french-racists_n_5aa45bade4b07047bec70239.

65 Transcript of Bannon's speech, under title "This is How Steve Bannon Sees the Entire World," provided by Buzzfeed: https://www.buzzfeed.com/lesterfeder/this-is-how-steve-bannon-sees-the-entire-world?utm_term=.eqDlyd89W#.ic7p79EzO Accessed May 15, 2017.

66 Teitelbaum, *War for Eternity*, 94.

67 Koffler, 151.

68 Green, 146.

69 Green, 148.
70 Koffler, 50.
71 Green, 236.
72 Christopher Wylie, *Mindf*ck: Cambridge Analytica and the Plot to Break America* (New York: Random House, 2019), 43.
73 Green, 143.
74 Wylie, *Mindf*ck*, 129.
75 Wylie, *Mindf*ck*, 127.
76 Wylie, *Mindf*ck*, 129–30.
77 Wylie, *Mindf*ck*, 144.
78 Wylie, *Mindf*ck*, 132.
79 Wylie, *Mindf*ck*, 132.
80 Teitelbaum, 193.
81 Wolin, *Heidegger in Ruins*.
82 Teitelbaum, 267.
83 Rosie Gray, "Get Out While You Can," *Buzzfeed*, May 1, 2019, https://www.buzzfeednews.com/article/rosiegray/katie-mchugh.
84 Omarosa Manigault Newman, *Unhinged: An Insider's Account of the Trump White House* (New York: Gallery Books, 2018), 184.
85 Emma-Kate Symons, "Steve Bannon Loves France," *Politico*, March 22, 2017, http://www.politico.eu/article/steve-bannons-french-marine-le-pen-front-national-donald-trump-far-right-populism-inspiration/.
86 Maya Kosoff, "Steve Bannon's Racist Comments About Silicon Valley Are Also Wildly Inaccurate," *Vanity Fair*, November 17, 2016, https://www.vanityfair.com/news/2016/11/steve-bannon-racist-comments-silicon-valley-inaccurate.
87 Matthew N. Lyons, *Insurgent Supremacists: The U.S. Far Right's Challenge to State and Empire* (Montreal: Kersplebedeb, 2018), xviii–ix.

Bibliography

Arnsdorf, Isaac, Doug Bock Clark, et al. "Heeding Steve Bannon's Call, Election Deniers Organize to Seize Control of the GOP—And Reshape America's Elections." *Pro Publica*, September 2, 2021. https://www.propublica.org/article/heeding-steve-bannons-call-election-deniers-organize-to-seize-control-of-the-gop-and-reshape-americas-elections.

Beiner, Ronald. *Dangerous Minds: Nietzsche, Heidegger, and the Return of the Far Right*. Philadelphia: University of Pennsylvania Press, 2018.

Bernstein, Joseph. "Here's How Breitbart and Milo Smuggled White Nationalism Into the Mainstream." *Buzzfeed*, October 5, 2017. https://www.buzzfeednews.com/article/josephbernstein/heres-how-breitbart-and-milo-smuggled-white-nationalism.

Berry, Damon T. *Blood and Faith: Christianity in American White Nationalism*. New York: Syracuse University Press, 2017.

Blumenthal, Paul and J.M. Rieger. "This Stunningly Racist French Novel is How Steve Bannon Explains the World." *Huffpost*, March 6, 2017. http://www.huffingtonpost.com/entry/steve-bannon-camp-of-the-saints-immigration_us_58b75206e4b0284854b3dc03.

Braune, Joan. "The Outsider as Insider: Steve Bannon, Fourth Turnings, and the Neofascist Threat." In Samir Gandesha, Ed., *Spectres of Fascism: Historical, Theoretical, and International Perspectives* (207–22). London: Pluto Press, 2020.

Crowley, Michael. "The Man Who Wants to Unmake the West." *Politico*, March 12, 2017. https://www.politico.eu/article/the-man-who-wants-to-unmake-the-west/.

Fahri, Paul. "How Breitbart Has Become a Dominant Voice in Conservative Media." *Washington Post*, June 10, 2017. https://www.washingtonpost.com/lifestyle/style/how-breitbart-has-become-a-dominant-voice-in-conservative-media/2016/01/27/a705cb88-befe-11e5-9443-7074c3645405_story.html?utm_term=.8ec77a9c6896.

Farrell, Nicholas. "'I'm Fascinated by Mussolini': Steve Bannon Talks Fascism." *The Spectator*, March 18, 2018. https://spectatorworld.com/topic/mussolini-steve-bannon/.

Farrell, Nicholas. "Steve Bannon on 'Masturbatory' Emmanuel Macron, Elites, and Old Etonians." *The Spectator World*, June 7, 2018, https://spectatorworld.com/topic/steve-bannon-rome/.

Gold, Matea, Rosalind S. Helderman, et al. "For Trump Adviser Stephen Bannon, Fiery Populism Followed Life in Elite Circles." *Washington Post*, November 19, 2016. https://www.washingtonpost.com/politics/for-trump-adviser-stephen-bannon-fiery-populism-followed-life-in-elite-circles/2016/11/19/de91ef40-ac57-11e6-977a-1030f822fc35_story.html?utm_term=.2a79678a5532.

Gray, Rosie. "Get Out While You Can." *Buzzfeed*, May 1, 2019. https://www.buzzfeednews.com/article/rosiegray/katie-mchugh.

Green, Joshua. *Devil's Bargain: Steve Bannon, Donald Trump, and the Storming of the Presidency.* New York: Penguin, 2017.

Helderman, Rosalind S. and Josh Dawsey, et al., "How Former Trump Adviser Steve Bannon Joined Forces with a Chinese Billionaire Who Has Divided the President's Allies." *Washington Post*, September 13, 2020, https://www.washingtonpost.com/politics/steve-bannon-guo-wengui/2020/09/13/8b43cd06-e964-11ea-bc79-834454439a44_story.html.

Howe, Neil. "Where Did Steve Bannon Get His Worldview? From My Book." *The Washington Post*, February 24, 2017. https://www.washingtonpost.com/entertainment/books/where-did-steve-bannon-get-his-worldview-from-my-book/2017/02/24/16937f38-f84a-11e6-9845-576c69081518_story.html.

Hurley, Ben. "Me and Li – Why I Left Falun Gong After Being a Devoted Believer for a Decade." *Medium*, October 22, 2017. https://ben-d-hurley.medium.com/-10677166298b.

Jacobs, Jennifer (@JenniferJJacobs). "The Last Man." October 20, 2017. https://twitter.com/JenniferJJacobs/status/921356724459753472.

Klayman, Alison, dir. *The Brink*. AliKlay Productions, RYOT films, 2019. Amazon. com.

Koffler, Keith. *Bannon: Always the Rebel*. Washington, DC: Regnery Publishing, 2017.

Kosoff, Mara. "Steve Bannon's Racist Comments about Silicon Valley Are Also Wildly Inaccurate." *Vanity Fair*, November 17, 2016. https://www.vanityfair.com/news/2016/11/steve-bannon-racist-comments-silicon-valley-inaccurate.

Last, John. "How 'Hobbit Camps' Rebirthed Italian Fascism." *Atlas Obscura*, October 3, 2017. https://www.atlasobscura.com/articles/hobbit-camps-fascism-italy.

Life Course Associates. "Our Clients." March 18, 2017. http://www.lifecourse.com/about/clients.html.

Life Course Associates. "Military." April 19, 2017. http://www.lifecourse.com/practice/military.html.

Lyons, Matthew N. *Insurgent Supremacists: The U.S. Far Right's Challenge to State and Empire.* Montreal: Kersplebedeb, 2018.

Maas, Peter. "Birth of a Radical: White Fear in the White House: Young Bannon Disciple Julia Hahn is a Case Study in Extremism." *The Intercept*, May 7, 2017. https://theintercept.com/2017/05/07/white-fear-in-the-white-house-young-bannon-disciple-julia-hahn-is-a-case-study-in-extremism/.

MacLean, Nancy. *Democracy in Chains: The Deep History of the Radical Right's Stealth Plan for America*. New York: Penguin, 2017.

Mantyla, Kyle. "Steve Bannon Wants Conservative Christian Poll Workers 'Inside the Room for the Knife Fight.'" *Right Wing Watch*, August 16, 2022. https://www.rightwingwatch.org/post/steve-bannon-wants-conservative-christian-poll-workers-inside-the-room-for-the-knife-fight/.

Meanwhile in China. "Mr. Wengui and Steve Bannon Make a Blood Oath to Destroy China." *YouTube*, June 14, 2020. https://www.youtube.com/watch?v=sdTi5HglO4g.

Morris, Errol, dir. *American Dharma*. Utopia, 2002.

Newman, Omarosa Manigault. *Unhinged: An Insider's Account of the Trump White House*. New York: Gallery Books, 2018.

Papenfuss, Mary. "Steve Bannon: 'Let Them Call You Racist; Wear It as a Badge of Honor." *Huffpost*, March 10, 2018. https://www.huffpost.com/entry/bannon-far-right-french-racists_n_5aa45bade4b07047bec70239.

Pearce, Matt. "Steve Bannon Found Influences in Ancient Thinkers, Reagan, and Nazi Propaganda." *Los Angeles Times*, December 9, 2016. http://www.latimes.com/nation/la-na-bannon-influences-20161209-story.html.

Purdy, Jedediah. "The Anti-Democratic Worldview of Steve Bannon and Peter Thiel." *Politico*, November 30, 2016, https://www.politico.com/magazine/story/2016/11/donald-trump-steve-bannon-peter-thiel-214490.

Radosh, Ronald. "Steve Bannon, Trump's Top Guy, Told Me He's a 'Leninist.'" *Daily Beast*, https://www.thedailybeast.com/steve-bannon-trumps-top-guy-told-me-he-was-a-leninist.

Red Scare podcast. "War Room Red Scare w/ Steve Bannon." April 4, 2020, July 9, 2021. https://redscarepodcast.libsyn.com/war-room-red-scare-w-steve-bannon.

Sedgwick, Mark. *Against the Modern World*. Oxford: Oxford University Press, 2004.

Stan, Adele. "Insurrectionist in Chief." *New Republic*, March 10, 2021. https://newrepublic.com/article/161574/steve-bannon-capitol-riots-insurrectionist-chief.

Strauss, William and Neil Howe. *The Fourth Turning: What the Cycles of History Tell Us About America's Next Rendezvous with Destiny*. New York: Broadway Books, 1997.

Suebsaeng, Asawin. "Steve Bannon Calls Jared Kushner a 'Cuck' and 'Globalist' Behind His Back." *Daily Beast*, May 5, 2017. https://www.thedailybeast.com/steve-bannon-calls-jared-kushner-a-cuck-and-globalist-behind-his-back.

Suebsaeng, Asawin. "Steve Bannon's Long Love Affair with War." *Daily Beast*, April 11, 2017. https://www.thedailybeast.com/steve-bannons-long-love-affair-with-war.

Symons, Emma-Kate. "Steve Bannon Loves France." *Politico*, March 22, 2017. http://www.politico.eu/article/steve-bannons-french-marine-le-pen-front-national-donald-trump-far-right-populism-inspiration/.

Teitelbaum, Benjamin R. "Collaborating with the Radical Right: Scholar-Informant Solidarity and the Case for an Immoral Anthropology." *Current Anthropology* 60, no. 3 (June 2019): 413–35.

Teitelbaum, Benjamin R. *War for Eternity: Inside Bannon's Far-Right Circle of Global Power Brokers*. New York: HarperCollins, 2020.

Tolentino, Jia. "Stepping Into the Uncanny, Unsettling World of Shen Yun." *The New Yorker*, March 19, 2019. https://www.newyorker.com/culture/culture-desk/stepping-into-the-uncanny-unsettling-world-of-shen-yun.

Van Zylen-Wood, Simon. "MAGA-land's Favorite Newspaper." *The Atlantic*, January 31, 2021. https://www.theatlantic.com/politics/archive/2021/01/inside-the-epoch-times-a-mysterious-pro-trump-newspaper/617645/?fbclid=IwAR3MW aAgU6B0SCl8TlmYLEe36TnrttTEm5mK_w_2_ZX-eRtuoiNxpYGi4zY

Wolff, Michael. *Fire and Fury: Inside the Trump White House*. New York: Henry Holt and Company, 2018.

Wolin, Richard. *Heidegger in Ruins: Between Philosophy and Ideology*. New Haven, CT: Yale University Press, 2022.

Wylie, Christopher. *Mindf*ck: Cambridge Analytica and the Plot to Break America*. New York: Random House, 2019.

4

LIMITATIONS OF THE "COUNTERING EXTREMISM" MODEL

We have now explored both individual-psychological and social-ideological dimensions of contemporary U.S. fascist movements, showing the need for both frames of analysis. In confronting the limitations of an overly individualized and psychologized model of confronting fascism, we must problematize such concepts as "extremism" and "radicalization." Classifying fascism as a form of "extremism" or "radicalism" enables fascistic state policies and empowers the far-right to attack the left, as well as bolstering Islamophobia. The theoretical framework of extremism and radicalization is supported by overlapping "counter-extremism" and "deradicalization" industries that involve some former fascists, government agencies, think tanks, law enforcement, counselors and social workers, and academics.

In addition, it is necessary to explore the limitations of the deradicalization industry's rhetorical trope that I call the "compassion narrative," a discourse that presents "compassion" as the primary tool for defeating hate. Overcoming fascism as *a social movement seeking power, always already connected to sources of power*, requires more than an individualized process of fascists' conversion, and it is not the duty of communities under threat to facilitate such conversions. The "compassion narrative," which depicts outreach from members of marginalized groups as the solution to fascism, serves as damaging advice to community activists, places unreasonable pressures on targets of hate, centers white perpetrators, and empowers far-right discourses of victim-blaming.

As I will make clear, I am not saying that compassionate outreach to fascists who are doubting their beliefs, to those being recruited into fascist movements, or to those in the process of leaving fascist ideology behind, always indicates sympathy for fascism or a lack of loyalty to fascism's victims. Indeed,

DOI: 10.4324/9781003031604-5

there is a place for work by those with appropriate skill sets in disengaging fascists from their movements and ideology, but this chapter is devoted to a critique of the ways in which the deradicalization industry fails to achieve solidarity with targeted communities, misunderstands fascist movements, and, in some respects, empowers fascism more than countering it.

Limitations of an "Extremism" Framework

Confronting the problem of fascism today requires surmounting the language of "extremism" and "radicalization" and the theoretical limitations of this terminology and schema. The extremism/radicalization schema (1) provides cover to the neoliberal political "center" by blaming racism and hate on a bizarre societal fringe and ignoring structures and policies that coincide with fascist aims; (2) pairs the left and the right together, enabling collaboration by "counter-extremists" with the state in targeting the left; and (3) enables and spreads Islamophobia, since Muslims have been racially and religiously coded as "extremists."

First, it is problematic to theorize fascism as a form of "extremism" or "radicalism" because it can *let the center off the hook*, failing to show how the demands of fascists harmonize with long-established structures and political policies. The actions of "fringe" fascist groups or even right-wing political parties cannot be solely blamed for the racist policies of the neoliberal center. In the United States, the child separation policy at the U.S.–Mexico border under Trump's presidency was shocking in its brutality and lack of empathy, but Republicans are not wrong to point out that Obama's and Biden's administrations also placed immigrant children of color in cages. In Europe as well as the United States, harsh policies of immigrant and refugee exclusion and mistreatment by politically centrist European governments, while coinciding with fascist or far-right aims, often arise to shore up economic globalization;[1] bigotry and violent state repression against immigrants of color assist in creating an underclass of demoralized, vulnerable foreign workers whose numbers can be constantly adjusted to meet the demands of the capitalist economy. The same is true of the way in which other populations, especially Black and indigenous U.S. Americans, are often sorted back and forth between the categories of exploited workforce and incarcerated masses. Furthermore, fascism is, as we have seen, a social movement seeking power and always already connected to sources of power. Even in countries where the far-right does not hold significant political offices, fascism draws power and protection from allies within, policies of, and central narratives of centers of political power. These allies include not only some politicians but also various powerful political funders, think tanks, media organs, and some members of law enforcement, the intelligence establishment, and the armed forces. The relationship between fascist movements and neoliberal centrist power structures is thus symbiotic; each feeds on the other, though neither is merely an outgrowth of the other. Fascists do pose a legitimate threat on their own, a threat that is political and not merely criminal, and they are not merely a symbolic representation of the state's already fascist character—they also can be insurgents that neoliberal power structures perceive as potential threats. Likewise, it is also the case that neoliberal centrist governments themselves originate racist, xenophobic, and otherwise discriminatory and dehumanizing policies that sustain mainstream structures of oppression that have long existed, still undefeated, in Western political states. Painting the far-right as radical and fringe can obscure the ways in which it already holds power, including political offices, in some cases, or the ways in which its aims are already being achieved independently of their own organizing.[2]

By defending a theoretical framework that presents fascists as "extremists," neoliberal power structures lend credence to fascists' own ideas. For example, the European "Exit" model of bringing people out of hate groups was built on a theory criticized by Liz Fekete, Director of the Institute of Race Relations in the United Kingdom, who calls the theory "white grievance."[3] White grievance theory partly agrees with fascist ideology about the causes of fascists' distress—seeing immigration, for example, as driving economic crisis and disenfranchisement of the "white working class," which is said to have "legitimate grievances," by which it is meant not merely that they are genuinely suffering from something in their lives but that they are at least partly correct about their assessment of the political sources of their suffering. Today, the European Commission of the European Union is heavily involved in promoting Exit programs in Europe, and white grievance theory fits easily and shifts anger away from capitalism to racialized minorities. In fact, the European Union has been involved in aggressive anti-immigrant enforcement, even in sub-Saharan Africa, and involved in numerous human rights violations.[4] Hence, in some cases, the very institutions that might fall under the far-right's denunciations of "globalism" (an antisemitic trope used to condemn both capitalist globalization and leftist international solidarity) are helping to promote far-right ideology.

Second, in addition to letting neoliberal power structures off the hook by blaming a convenient bogeyman, painting fascism as fringe "extremism" allows for a *facile equation between the left and the right*. Under this framework, leftist ideologies (such as socialism, communism, and anarchism) can be painted as somehow equivalent to fascism and organized racism, with both the left and the right labeled as "extremism" or "radicalism." Left and right are then seen as locked in a cycle of "polarization," and the center is painted as the location of safety and sanity, with the extremes as the source of violence, conflict, and political division. This way of thinking has a long history, with the condemnation of slavery abolitionists, labor leaders, and others as "extremists." It is seen in Cold War rhetoric as well, which painted

Western capitalist states as the alternative to the extremes of fascism and communism, and it paved the way for COINTELPRO, the FBI's mass surveillance, infiltration, violence against and criminalization of left wing, heavily people of color-led, social movements in the 1960s.[5] One COINTELPRO category of alleged extremists was entitled by the J. Edgar Hoover's FBI "Black Hate" and included the Rev. Dr. Martin Luther King, Jr. and the Southern Christian Leadership Conference and the Student Nonviolent Coordinating Committee (SNCC), among others.[6]

The trend of using "extremism" frames against the left also continues into the present, for example, with the FBI recently classifying antifascists and a nebulous category of "Black identity extremists" as terrorists, while right-wingers, including Trump, clamored that "Antifa" should be labeled a "terrorist organization." On May 31, 2020, Trump's Attorney General William Barr released a statement that "peaceful and legitimate protests have been hijacked by violent radical elements" and that "outside radicals and agitators," including "Antifa," were "exploiting the situation to pursue their own separate, violent, and extremist agenda."[7] On June 26, Barr instituted a task force on countering "anti-government extremists," under which he included both "Antifa" and the right-wing "Boogaloo" circle, which is calling for hastening societal collapse and civil war.[8]

Likewise, the appeals of police departments for special gear or other resources targeted at dealing with white supremacist extremist threats can be easily mobilized against people of color, especially Blacks, and leftist activists, who are targeted more frequently by police violence than the far-right is. (And the far-right frequently finds ways to mobilize the role of policing against people of color and the left, for example, by "swatting"—calling in fake threats to endanger the lives of targets by mobilizing police SWAT teams against them.) How quickly and dramatically police and paramilitary forces can mobilize against activists was made again apparent in many cities across America in the 2020 Black Lives Matter protests. In many cases, far-right or fascist armed militia members patrolled or intimidated protests with the tacit permission of police, who also turned against anti-racism protesters with gear allegedly designed to target "extreme" or "terrorist" activity. Protesters were met with rubber bullets, tear gas, sound grenades, and so on by police and targeted by car attacks, beatings, and other acts of aggression and violence by the far-right. Emboldened self-deputizing racist militias have been widely tolerated or encouraged by police across the country at Black Lives Matter protests and demonstrations against coronavirus-related safety precautions. (This is particularly frightening for an assessment of U.S. politics, given that some look for the use of "paramilitary" forces as evidence of fascism.)

The equation between left and right that makes it possible to target the left as "extreme" is often enabled by "horseshoe theory." According to horseshoe theory, the further left or right one goes on the political spectrum, the more one approaches the opposite extreme, with very far-left and very far-right political movements being almost indistinguishable. Horseshoe theory has a number of a problems, but among the most prominent is that it ignores the problem that Alexander Reid Ross calls "fascist creep":[9] fascism is always appropriating from, and trying to infiltrate, the left. That fascism attempts to blur the lines between left and right does not mean, however, that fascism is inherently left-wing, any more than say, Steve Bannon is inherently a Hindu (for appropriating Hindu concepts via Julius Evola, as discussed in the previous chapter). An elementary examination of the history of fascism in Europe in the 1930s should make this very clear—leftists were among the first victims of fascist genocide and its strongest opponents. ("First they came for the Communists," Pastor Niemoller's famous saying begins.) Today fascists continue to target the left, whether through violent street brawls or the disruption of events and activities, online and in person.

Horseshoe theory has a long history, and equations of fascism and communism could be seen as early as the 1920s.[10] What "extremism" and "radicalization" do for descriptions of individuals involved in both left and right, political theories of "totalitarianism" as well as "populism" often do for broader social movements and political philosophies. Theories of totalitarianism and populism tend to paint both communism and fascism, among other ideologies, as manifestations of the same fundamental tendencies.[11] Totalitarianism theories stress authoritarian power to the exclusion of other ideological components, while theories of populism focus on the use of a rhetoric that pits the people against the "elites," a rhetoric that is deployed both by the left and by the right but for very different reasons. (In the case of Steve Bannon's "populist" rhetoric, for example, as in the case of much far-right populist rhetoric, populism may be simply a tool to gain popular support for anti-democratic, illiberal, and elitist political ends, and this is widely the case with many far-right "populist" parties and movements.)

Initiatives against extremism, often government-funded with counterterrorism money, walk a tightrope between demonizing the left and standing in solidarity with the left against fascist extremists who victimize minorities. This ultimately makes solidarity with the living targets or victims of fascism difficult-to-impossible for those who rely on an "extremism" model. Hewing to the "center," these approaches are likely to condemn "extremism" on both the left and the right. The attempt to combat both left and right extremism becomes more problematic when it surpasses mere rhetoric and collaborates with government entities or the far-right to surveil or crack down on the left.

Despite these problems, the rhetoric of "extremism" when used to describe the far-right is often well-intentioned, and it is used by groups like the Southern Poverty Law Center (SPLC), which does good work fighting hate. However, the use of this language by mainline national non-profits fighting hate groups, like SPLC, the Anti-Defamation League (ADL), and the

Simon Wiesenthal Center,[12] is not unproblematic and may, in fact, relate to a willingness to collaborate with law enforcement approaches. In particular, the ADL and Wiesenthal Center have promoted right-wing agendas. For example, operating under a countering "extremism" model, the ADL has collaborated with law enforcement, law enforcement informants, and far-right groups to keep files on leftist organizations and to promote right-wing policies. Although the ADL is often charged by left activists (including many Jews) with silencing leftist critics of Israel, its historic collaboration with the right extends still further, including working against critics of U.S. intervention into Central America in the 1980s, utilizing FBI informants, and relying on far-right sources for information.[13] Beginning in the 1960s, an ADL informant in San Francisco, who also spied for the FBI, "sold information on anti-apartheid activists to both South African agents and ADL."[14] The informant, Roy Bullock, also gathered information on left-leaning groups including Greenpeace, the National Association for the Advancement of Colored People (NAACP), and Act Up.[15] In the 1960s through 1980s, the ADL relied on information from John Rees and Sheila Rees, including their *Information Digest*, a "secret newsletter sent to clients ranging from the New York State Police to the FBI to the John Birch Society."[16] In the 1980s under Reagan, *Political Research Associates* reports:

> ADL joined a network of conservative and Christian Right groups and government intelligence agencies to covertly plan and carry out a domestic propaganda campaign to bolster public support for Reagan administration Central America policies. This effort was part of a larger campaign designed by CIA director William Casey, Oliver North, and others to use private groups, such as the [Rees-affiliated] Western Goals Foundation, to carry out domestic propaganda functions to support foreign covert intelligence operations.[17]

It is not surprising that organizations relying on some version of "horseshoe theory" would engage in activities countering the left, even, for example, leftist activism against racist apartheid in South Africa. After all, horseshoe theory contributes to victim-blaming by framing the left and the right as not only similar to each other but also mutually reinforcing. Those on the front lines of left-wing struggle and thus most likely to be targeted by the far-right are painted as equivalent to the far-right, seen as extremists and even as causal of the far-right's own violence against them. This victim-blaming conveniently fits the far-right's own narratives. Going further, members of the far-right may even present themselves as "extremism experts" as a means to target the left.

Take the case of Jack Buckby, a former member of the British National Party, which was founded by Nazis. Buckby has reinvented himself as a former extremist and "counter-extremism researcher" and has published a book, titled *Monster of Their Own Making: How the Far-Left, Media, and Politicians Are Creating Far-Right Extremists*. From Buckby, who claims to be renouncing a white nationalist past, we learn that "I was a member of a nationalist political party with neo-Nazi roots that attracted the votes of a million desperate, working class British people who had no other option."[18] Buckby sees immigration into the United Kingdom as creating a crisis that is driving people to the far-right; thus, he continues to blame immigrants for social problems as he did before, but now he has widened the umbrella of problems to include the "far-right" itself (a category in which he conveniently includes only self-titled Nazis). This use of far-right talking points to allegedly transcend both the far-right and the left is a frequent problem, which is made possible by counter-extremism discourses.

In addition to providing political cover to the center and labeling the left as extreme, the "extremism"/"radicalization" model of analysis *enables Islamophobia*. Today, Muslims are frequently lumped in with white supremacists and leftist activists as "extremists." In a schema that is rather typical, for example, the German government lists four kinds of extremism that it tracks: "right-wing extremism," "left-wing extremism," "extremism of foreigners (excluding Islamism)," and "Islamism and Islamist terrorism."[19] By linking the left, the far-right, and Muslims as extremist threats, the centrist power structures of Europe and North America are then portrayed as neutral bastions of calm, which they counter-pose to the ethnic or religious identities of the Middle Eastern countries those governments wish to bomb. A summary of this mentality was offered by theologian William T. Cavanaugh: "*Their* violence is…irrational and fanatical. *Our* violence, being secular, is…peace making."[20] Furthermore, painting Muslims as extremists enables Islamophobic policies, such as the Trump administration's "Muslim ban," initiated by white nationalist Trump advisor Stephen Miller.

As with its impact on left movements through horseshoe theory, the "extremism" and "radicalization" model spurs victim-blaming against Muslim communities and contributes to Islamophobia. For example, it has become par for the course in certain circles to blame fundamentalist Muslim clerics in the United Kingdom for the formation of the English Defence League (EDL), a violent Islamophobic hate group. Political scientist Roger Eatwell coined the term "cumulative extremism" to describe the ways in which conflicting types of "extremism" can play off one another and increase the extremism of each.[21] While this may be a phenomenon that occurs, placing stress on this mutual causality can feed into institutional and systemic discourses of victim-blame while reductively overlooking more significant factors in the causation of prejudice that pre-exist the mutual interplay of "extreme" groups. Cumulative extremism and a similar term, "reciprocal radicalization," are concepts perpetuated since then by establishment deradicalization agencies and leaders, such as those involved in the United Kingdom's Prevent or the United States' "Countering Violent Extremism" (CVE) initiatives. (Under Biden's administration, the official U.S. Department of Homeland Security office devoted to CVE has been renamed the Center for Prevention Programs and Partnerships.)

To make clear how easily linked the theory of cumulative extremism is to victim-blaming, replace the EDL and fundamentalist Muslim clerics with another example. Consider, for example, the rightful outrage that would likely result if any leading expert on hate crime and "extremism" were to, for example, blame certain Jews (such as the Israeli military, or even Jewish "extremist" groups in Israel) for "radicalizing" the Pittsburgh synagogue shooter. In response, such an expert would face significant censure from others in their field, and rightly so. Why, especially considering that such violent antisemitic shooters sometimes cite the actions of Israel as among their motivations for violence? Such talk is antisemitism, not because it is critical of Israel but because it blames Jews for hate crimes against Jews and because it equates all Jews with one another and with Israel. Only antisemites are responsible for antisemitic hate, and only Islamophobes are responsible for Islamophobic hate. However, Islamophobic victim-blaming routinely gets a pass among some extremism experts, and Muslims are rarely accorded the same level of acknowledgment of individual distinction and uniqueness by the counterterrorism industry, so discussing causal interaction with far-right Islamophobic groups and right-wing Muslim clerics bleeds over very easily into agencies and pundits blaming Muslims for their own victimization.

Tracing the origins of Islamophobic narratives in counter-extremism discourses would require a heavy investigation of War on Terror rhetoric as well as how that rhetoric has seeped into the work of various non-governmental organizations (NGOs), including those that allegedly pursue non-policing interventions. With regard to the United Kingdom, a piece of the story to be explored would also no doubt be the role of recently closed government-funded deradicalization project Quilliam, co-founded by Maajid Nawaz (a former member of fundamentalist Muslim group Hizb ut-Tahrir), who has been accused of promoting Islamophobia.[22] It would also require looking at how Islamophobic hate groups often mimic the rhetoric of state-funded entities and programs like Prevent and the sometimes tangled intersections between Islamophobic hate groups and programs designed to "counter extremism." An example of this can be seen in the collaboration of former white supremacists in the United States with the right-wing group Clarion Project.

In the United States, for example, former pro-Al Qaeda propagandist Jesse Morton of deradicalization group Light Upon Light; recent National Socialist Movement leader Jeff Schoep, who has founded his own deradicalization group called Beyond Barriers; and a few former white supremacists associated in the past or present with deradicalization groups, Life After Hate and Parents for Peace, associated themselves with the Clarion Project, appearing in videos, podcasts, or tabling with them at events. As of July 2020, Clarion Project was listed by the SPLC as an Islamophobic hate group.[23] The Clarion Project's campaigns include the distribution of millions of free copies of an anti-Muslim documentary DVD called *Obsession*, in the lead-up to the election of President Obama. Clarion Project is a right-wing group, painting not only Muslims but also left movements as extreme. In June 2020, for example, Clarion Project's Shireen Qudosi wrote of the Black Lives Matter protests:

> Whether they come for statues today or people tomorrow, the goal of any extremist movement is to rewrite the narrative by obliterating any other narrative. The goal of this current movement is no different. It isn't just to level racial injustice; it's to level America.[24]

The Clarion Project website has an "extremist map" that mimics the SPLC's famous "hate map" of hate groups across the United States. When I checked the listings for my current state, Washington State, I saw that Clarion had listed only three "extremist groups" in Washington, one of which was the state's chapter of the Muslim civil liberties group, the Council on American-Islamic Relations (CAIR), and the other two of which were simply places of worship (Islamic centers or mosques). For comparison, the SPLC's map at that time listed 30 hate groups in Washington State, including Atomwaffen Division, Feuerkrieg Division, American Identity Movement (Identity Evropa), Patriot Front, the Northwest Hammerskins, and the Wolves of Vinland, as well as a chapter of Islamophobic hate group (co-founded by then State Representative Matt Shea) Act for America.[25] Apparently even openly pro-terrorism accelerationist groups like Atomwaffen Division and Feuerkrieg Division were insufficiently "extreme" for Clarion's "extremist map."

The reasons for toleration of Islamophobia by experts on hate and extremism are multiple, but one reason is the dependence of experts on government counterterrorism funds, which suggests they either agree with narratives that frame Muslims in their countries as a dangerous radicalized threat or have financial incentive to go along with an Islamophobic discourse. The resources for countering Islamist terrorism far outmatch resources for countering fascist and white supremacist terrorism, although researchers in the latter area may also vie for funding from the same pools and be drawn into shared discourses. Expert on Islamophobia and its ties to the security state, Arun Kundnani, writes:

> Disraeli once remarked, at the high point of British colonial expansion, that "The East is a career"; today, "counter-radicalisation" is a career,

as young scholars enter the mini-industry of national security thinktanks, terrorism studies departments, law enforcement counterterrorism units and intelligence services to work on modelling radicalisation. Of course, scholars of political violence should want societies to make use of their work in order to reduce such violence, but true scholarship also involves a duty to question the underlying assumptions that define the discipline, particularly when those assumptions reflect the priorities of governments that are themselves parties to the conflict under investigation.[26]

Kundnani points out that discussion of foreign policy is almost never on the table in discussions of Islamist terrorism by counter-extremism experts. Lisa Stampnitzky writes that the counterterrorism field takes on "anti-knowledge characteristics"; the very self-designated "experts" on terrorism eschew many forms of knowledge, seeing terrorism simply as "evil" rather than as an object to be understood.[27]

A shift in counterterrorism to a focus on "radicalization" several years after 9/11 was greeted by some researchers as a liberal reform; rather than seeing Islamist terrorists as a faceless mob to be bombed out of existence, often-pro-imperialist reformers suggested a gentler approach, focusing on understanding the psychological conditions that give rise to violence and attempting to prevent Islamist terrorism through social work-type outreach and counter-messaging. However, as is frequently the case with reform efforts directed at fundamentally oppressive institutions—consider, for example, that the modern prison system is partly a product of reform campaigns against brutal corporal punishments and executions[28]—the attempt to reform counterterrorism led to new violations of rights and dignity. Ignoring political questions and focusing on Islamist terrorism as caused by a combination of "theology" and psychological factors, the counterterrorism industry bolstered oppressive profiling initiatives and surveillance. Programs like the United Kingdom's Prevent have been critiqued by numerous scholars and activists from "suspect communities," with youth and others being at risk of being reported to the government by teachers, therapists, and others required to watch for "warning signs" under faulty radicalization theories.[29] (Furthermore, although policies that demonize and discriminate against Muslims are wrong on their face, many argue that those policies may also be self-undermining[30]—after all, if a troubled young person reasonably believes that their religious leaders, teachers, therapists, and all other authority figures in their life would be required to report them to the police, who are they going to go to for help if they are having thoughts of enacting violence?)

The marshaling of extremism theory to the use of Islamophobia is enabled, in part, by the role of right-wing pro-Israel groups that have positioned themselves as defenders of Jews against antisemitism. Thus, for example, the Simon Wiesenthal Center defended the Trump administration's attempt to criminalize participation in "Antifa."[31] The Wiesenthal Center is hawkish and right-wing on foreign policy and supported the invasions of Afghanistan and Iraq.[32] Political theorist Wendy Brown studied the Wiesenthal Center's Museum of Tolerance, offering it as a case study in her argument that "tolerance" is "a contemporary discourse of depoliticization in which power and history make little or no appearance."[33] One of the museum's exhibits she critiques seemed to suggest a need to engage in "racial profiling" in light of "recent acts of terrorism...committed by Islamic extremists."[34]

The pro-Israel politics of anti-hate foundations like the ADL and Wiesenthal Center contributes to their overall failure to combat Islamophobia effectively by coloring their perception of mid-East politics. Those active in fighting antisemitism are often oppositional to or wary of Palestinian solidarity demands, and to be fair, a carefulness in understanding and acknowledging the reasons for that hesitancy is warranted. After all, the term "Zionists" becomes a catchall for Jews when used by white nationalists, who speak, for example, of the United States as "ZOG," a "Zionist Occupation Government," repeating a trope of secret Jewish control that erases the United States' own imperialist aims in the Middle East by imagining the United States as a manipulated pawn of Israel. Meanwhile, some groups professing a commitment to solidarity with Palestinians, such as Allison Weir's "If Americans Knew," have leaned on American nationalism, painting Israel as bad for "U.S. interests," while platforming or being platformed by white nationalists and even promoting antisemitic tropes, such as blood libel[35] (the age-old trope falsely claiming that Jews consume the blood of Christian children in religious rituals).

Despite these realities and the need to combat antisemitism, including when it comes presented in anti-Zionist packaging, a frequent collective failure by those engaged in the deradicalization and counter-extremism industries to engage in solidarity with Palestinians' struggles ultimately undermines work against antisemitism and empowers fascism. On a national scale, confusions are created about the meaning of antisemitism that allow far-right activists who traffic in antisemitic tropes to defend themselves by hiding behind their support for Israel. Internationally, we also see confusing political alliances, such as antisemitic[36] Hungarian Prime Minister Viktor Órban being welcomed to Israel by Benjamin Netanyahu and professing his support for Israel. The counter-extremism industry's inability to be in solidarity with Palestinians is further enabled by the understanding of "extremism" itself and how characterizations of "terrorism" have been historically shaped to target all forms of Palestinian resistance to Israeli occupation.

The U.S. left itself is not without blame in enabling the centrist division that allows the casting of the ordinary Muslim other as a "terrorist" alongside white supremacists. The U.S. left often fails to look at intersections between domestic and international struggles, in particular failing to see connections between U.S. imperialism abroad and structural white supremacy and settler colonialism at home.[37] One of the many lessons that needs to be learned from this is that understanding hate movements domestically cannot be uncoupled from an understanding of foreign policy issues; in the case of the United States, we cannot talk about white supremacy and settler colonialism effectively without also talking about U.S. imperialism (and vice versa). White progressives who focus on international peacemaking may neglect racial injustices in their backyard, for example. The Black Lives Matter movement, to its credit, has positioned itself as part of an international struggle, including citing its support for an end of the Occupation of Palestine. (This commitment has, in turn, contributed to Black Lives Matter being classed with its Muslim members and allies as "extremist" by groups like the Clarion Project.)

"Deradicalization" and Failures of Solidarity

"Deradicalization," as a scholar and practitioner field, took off following 9/11 and was fed by government terrorism prevention funds. Since prevention of Islamist terrorism and of white supremacist terrorism was fitted under the same umbrella, incentives for researchers and deradicalization experts to interpret Islamist and white supremacist terrorism as fundamentally similar were very high.

The melding of theories concerning Islamist and white supremacist terrorism also leads to a failure to condemn white nationalist ideology as fundamentally violent. Ironically, in an attempt to rein in Islamophobia, the deradicalization field established a distinction between radical beliefs and radical behavior, and some are increasingly emphasizing that only those whose *behavior* is likely to be radical/violent should be investigated. Because concepts of radicalization have been depoliticized to avoid criticism of neoconservative foreign policy, ideological "radicalization" of Muslims is generally described in religious as opposed to political terms. But since favoring a particular interpretation of Islam does not predict an intent to carry out violent attacks, the distinction between radical beliefs and radical behavior is intended to prevent the profiling of broad swaths of simply religiously practicing Muslims. However, since "Islamist radicalism" has now been equated with white nationalism and fascism, which are *inherently violent* ideologies unlike Islam, which is simply a religion subject to many interpretations like any other religion, a similar distinction is now being extended to fascists. The focus, it is said, should not be on those with "radical beliefs" (who happen to be fascists, white supremacists, etc.) but simply on those particular white nationalists and fascists who are the ones prone to "violent extremism." This distinction is not helpful when applied to fascists, however, because fascism glorifies violence as natural and good, and fascism's aims cannot be accomplished in society without a genocidal social program.

For example, the late Jesse Morton of Light Upon Light distinguished between radical beliefs and the use of violence, seeing the former as not necessarily a cause for concern. From a legal perspective, one would hope that law enforcement would distinguish between radical beliefs and violent behavior, not prosecuting or targeting anyone for mere beliefs. However, from the standpoint of civil society and certainly from the standpoint of social movements, the distinction between a "fascist radical" and an "actively violent fascist" is meaningless: promotion of white nationalism is always already violence, even when one is not committing violence of a prosecutable kind. Fascist propaganda is designed to scare, to tell people whose social status is already precarious that they will never fit in and never be safe, and to push policies that dehumanize and endanger others.

All profession of fascist belief is, of course, a profession of support for violence, but perhaps the distinction being made is roughly between those who pursue a "normalization" or "entryist" model, discussed in earlier chapters, and those who, such as accelerationist neo-Nazis, openly praise mass shooters and urge immediate acts of terrorism. Some in the counterterrorism world have even suggested working with fascist groups like the Proud Boys or Generation Identity to "counter violent extremism."[38] As discussed in previous chapters, as entryist approaches fail to achieve their goals, fascists often proceed to more openly violent approaches. If one waits to intervene with people being drawn into fascist ideology until they begin to openly espouse terrorist tactics—or worse, if one platforms or labels as "deradicalized" individuals who are still white nationalists but now "reject violent means"—the effectiveness of one's deradicalization program is significantly hampered.

In the United States, one of the ways the deradicalization industry intersects with government counterterrorism work is through the role of CVE programs (now TVTP, Targeted Violence and Terrorism Prevention). Although the deradicalization group Life After Hate lost a projected CVE grant offered by the Obama administration after Trump took office (with a new administration emphasis on treating "violent extremism" as a solely Muslim phenomenon), its grant was restored in the fall of 2020. Under the Biden administration, there was renewed hope by some other "anti-hate" or deradicalization groups of receiving government grants, some of which have received funding. As with its parallel in the United Kingdom, known as Prevent, in the United States, CVE has been critiqued for profiling Muslim communities.[39] The think tank, the Brennan Center for Justice, has tracked and critiqued CVE and TVTP for their impact on civil liberties, especially of Muslims.[40] The term "CVE" (along with PVE, Preventing Violent Extremism) is used loosely by the deradicalization field, sometimes to imply government funding and sometimes as a general descriptor. As a funded program, similarly to the perhaps even worse Prevent program in the United Kingdom, CVE encourages spying and surveillance of Muslim youth and targets Muslim youth of color, such as Somali communities in Minneapolis.[41] In addition, CVE has been used as a catchall category for anti-activist surveillance and investigation, as, for example, in the case of the Denver police department, which used CVE funds to track Black Lives Matter, LGBTQ+ activists, and refugees.[42] CVE has served a role in the construction of "suspect communities," and activist resistance to it, including its related deradicalization industry, has mounted.[43]

Discourses of the Deradicalization Industry

The deradicalization industry's professed enemies are "extremism," "radicalism," "terrorism," and "polarization." Its professed friends are "tolerance," "empathy," "compassion," and "forgiveness." By placing the emphasis on the perpetrator of hate, the deradicalization industry ignores both society's guilt and victims' needs.[44] It looks for hate at the "extremes" and seeks to ameliorate that hate with kindness to and dialogue with haters. Although it professes a commitment to accountability for perpetrators and speaks out against racism and other forms of hate in at least general terms, the outward message to non-"extremists" seems to be focused on preparing society to forgive and welcome back "formers" (former members of hate groups or other "extremist" groups). Victims of hate crime (never mind leaders of anti-racist movements, who are nearly never mentioned or interacted with) appear as supporting characters, if ever, in the deradicalization industry's narratives; generally speaking, the dead ones are most advantageous to the deradicalization industry, whose members frequently release statements or speak at forums following mass shootings and other atrocities, expressing their remorse and pain over the suffering inflicted by violent hate. While this regret is generally sincere, and probably painful to express, the more challenging work lies in speaking with people impacted by hate, especially those who are encountered not as passive objects of violence but who can challenge the deradicalization field to look deeper at its thinking, its discourses, and its failures of solidarity.

Deradicalization models generally exhibit the problems inherent in the overly individualized, psychologized analysis of fascism—one of the two chief errors in analysis and strategy this book addresses. In brief, deradicalization models, even at their most sincere and compassionate, tend to elide the following truths:

- Fascism is a social movement seeking power, always already connected to sources of power. Vying for funding from offices headed up by people like far-right Sebastian Gorka's wife, in the United States in the Trump administration, for example, puts one in the awkward position of determining whether one can speak about the Trump administration's own alliances with fascism and its inherent white nationalism, without losing one's potential funding source.

- Fascism comes with social benefits. Many of the leading former hate group members in today's deradicalization field were active in the 1980s and 1990s racist skinhead movements or similar gang-like hate groups; they engaged in pitched street battles or other violent crimes and knew that they were signing up for possible imprisonment or dying in the "race war." Yet it has always been true that fascism can be a path to power, and it is truer today than it has been for some time; young people joining fascist movements may not be signing up to be criminalized or killed—in fact, they might be envisioning bright futures in media, politics, or law enforcement. However, the deradicalization industry focuses on theorizing these individuals as alienated and traumatized, existing at the "extremes" of society, and on a path to nowhere.
- Fascists believe what they say, as much as can be expected of participants in any ideology, and they are truly racists and hateful. As noted in Chapter 1, I agree in large part with those who believe that people join such movements in pursuit of meaning and identity. However, it is often the case that formers looking backward on their involvement see themselves, or present themselves, as having been merely followers seeking to fill psychological needs, and this elides the reality of the deep racism already present in U.S. society; in fact, "formers" were probably racists before joining fascist or white nationalist groups. When white supremacists claim that many white people already privately or unconsciously believe what they openly preach, they are sadly not wrong. The frequent presentation of members of hate groups by the deradicalization industry as psychologically damaged criminals confuses the public.[45] For example, journalists continue to express shock at how "normal" Nazis turn out to be and report on their grocery shopping routines, fashion choices, and video game hobbies with amazement. The sooner we as a society can realize the extent to which fascism rests upon social structures and institutions we regard as normal, the sooner we can confront those structures to prevent the perpetuation of fascist movements.
- Fascists generally initially leave their movements because life gets overwhelmingly hard for them, not because they have changed their beliefs, which tends to happen later if at all. Consequently, tactics like deplatforming, ostracism, and doxxing of fascists are not necessarily counter to deradicalization, even though deradicalization is not their aim. Aggressive and confrontational tactics that make it difficult for fascists to accomplish their goals can leave them stymied and depressed and do not automatically lead to escalation to terrorism, but such tactics are routinely discouraged by the deradicalization industry in favor of more "compassionate" ones. For example, in his book *Breaking Hate*, Christian Picciolini acknowledges in

one chapter that a former member of Atomwaffen Division reached out to him for help leaving the movement because he had been doxxed,[46] which would seem to indicate the effectiveness of more aggressive tactics. Yet Picciolini complains in another chapter that a community that put up fliers warning people that a white nationalist (who had allegedly privately disengaged from organized hate, though this was not known to the public if so) had moved into the neighborhood was engaged in judgmental "virtue signaling"[47] that would make it harder for people to leave hate groups. (By the way, a number of the formers I am quoting critically in this chapter, Picciolini among them, are sincere and have helped people. In Picciolini's case, he was also one of the few "professional formers" who publicly critiqued the Trump administration's role in promoting white nationalism, and he has called out the problem of deradicalization groups often being "right-wing grant mills."[48] Pushing "compassionate" tactics is the norm among formers in deradicalization work; I see the problem as systemic and structural, not a matter of a "few bad apples" but a problem with the hegemonic discourse and cultural milieu of the deradicalization scene.)

- A final critique of the deradicalization model: the protection of vulnerable communities must come first and never be put in second place to a mission of conversion of haters. Although the deradicalization field might superficially agree with this statement, most experts in the field appear to have given very little thought to methods of protecting communities endangered by those they seek to help (although they are often helping people who have already decided to leave their movements rather than conducting "interventions"). Protection of potential targets is typically viewed as a task for law enforcement, a conclusion that makes sense given the frequent closeness of deradicalization projects to government-led programs but a conclusion that is naïve considering the relationship between law enforcement and vulnerable communities. (Many of those most likely to be targeted by fascists, such as immigrants, Black and indigenous people, Muslims, members of the LGBTQ+ community, and outspoken leftist activists, among others, often face violence or mistreatment by police.)

Many of these problems stem from alliances (whether formal or informal) with government institutions and a comparative lack of relationship and trust with left-wing activists, especially in communities of color; this social positioning of the deradicalization field affixes it firmly within the discourse of "extremism" and its accompanying limitations. "Deradicalization" organizations and networks that seek to help people leave hate groups and other "violent extremist" groups (such as ISIS) tend to rely on theories that stress fascism as "extremism," that blame the left for "polarization," and that hold to a horseshoe theory of the relationship between the left and the right. This theoretical framing gives rise to *failures of solidarity*—for example, some of the social media accounts of leading figures in the deradicalization space leaped to "humanize" police rather than to defend the Black Lives Matter movement in the summer of 2020. (As the very debate between the slogans "Black Lives Matter" and "All Lives Matter" points up, while all human beings have dignity and worth, choosing to defend the dehumanized in their particularity is the mark of commitment to that very universality of dignity.)

The reasons for the deradicalization establishment's embrace of the rhetoric of extremism, polarization, and horseshoe theory are multiple. Among them is simply the psychological and political confusion in the field caused by the presence of many former fascists and former white supremacists in deradicalization leadership. It is certainly possible to leave hate movements and genuinely transform one's worldview and behavior, although it can take many years to unwind the conditioning. However, formers do tend to have certain limitations of experience, worldview, and habit, which can make it difficult for them to empathize intellectually with the communities they once harmed, and which can leave them struggling to understand the difference between marginalized communities *being afraid* or being merely *offended*, *protecting themselves* or *being aggressive*, and *angrily protesting righteously* or *spreading hate meaninglessly*.

Some formers also struggle to understand the worldview of leftist social movements and the reasons for the left's choices of tactics and strategies. For example, some former neo-Nazi skinheads who once tussled with "Antifa" in the streets emphasize that antifascist tactics could never have deradicalized them and, in fact, only made their views more entrenched during their time in the movement—thus, they suggest, such tactics should be abandoned. The error in this argument is that it rests on a misunderstanding of what antifascist tactics are intended to achieve. As Aristotle correctly argued over two millennia ago, in order to fairly judge the success of a project, one must know its intended ends. A fair critic does not judge a horror film for failing to be a romantic comedy nor condemn a carpenter making a desk for having made a "bad chair." Antifascism is not a deradicalization program—it is aimed at the protection of vulnerable communities and the defeat of fascism. If these ends can be accomplished without changing the hearts of individual fascists, antifascism can still achieve its aim. It seeks not to *convert* but to *disempower* fascists and their organizations, by denying them spaces, platforms, and access to all forms of power and influence. Antifascism perhaps echoes the sentiments of Kwame Ture (Stokely Carmichael), who famously said, "If a white man wants to lynch me, that's his problem. If he has the power to lynch me, that's my problem. Racism is not a question of attitude; it's a question of power."

I must confess that I find the aims of antifascism simple to understand, and I struggle to comprehend why some former fascists seem to misunderstand them so frequently, to such a degree that I suspect some of them of being deliberately dense. However, their process of healing and confronting their past can orient formers in a frame of reference emphasizing the redemption of perpetrators rather than solidarity with the marginalized. Granted, overcoming fascism as a society is in certain respects a redemptive project ("repair of the world"), since fascism is rooted in human and spiritual problems that require the transformation and redemption of individuals through facing the voids in their lives and society and seeking the truth with patience. However, the narratives and ideology of the deradicalization field, and especially of its leading "formers," make errors in this attempt, including by propagating narratives and approaches that center the experience of perpetrators rather than the targets of fascism and the protagonists of antifascist struggle. This can be understood even from within the frame of an individualized, criminological model that honors restorative justice: proper restorative justice centers and empowers victims, not perpetrators. Restorative justice's empathy for victims *can* help transform perpetrators, but this active empathy can be easily lost by a deradicalization model heavily focused on rehabilitation, healing, and forgiveness for perpetrators rather than reparations to victims.

Deradicalization and the "Extremism" Framework

Because of the closeness of deradicalization projects to government counterterrorism networks and funding, the deradicalization field is more likely to be rooted in an "extremism" framework, recapitulating such tropes as horseshoe theory as a result of being surrounded by this language and theory at all times and hearing far less from leftist social movements on the front lines of struggles against structural injustice. Deradicalization programs rely on the extremism/polarization framing for the achievement of grants and advancement. Furthermore, good relationships with government agencies may provide risky deradicalization efforts some sense of safety as well as the possibility of arranging some degree of protection for individuals seeking to leave movements (which is not to say that deradicalization programs are simply shielding formers from legal accountability, although this may be the case with some[49]).

Furthermore, the history of programs aimed at the deradicalization of neo-Nazis is fraught with collaboration with the far-right and failures of solidarity with fascism's victims. In the lead-up to the official founding of Exit Sweden, one of the first programs for deradicalization of neo-Nazis,

> naïve social workers at the centre were offering neo-nazi skinheads "fun" activities such as military and supervisory guard training and coach trips to White Power music concerts across Sweden (racist concerts were also held on the premises), as well as courses in desktop publishing and newspaper production.[50]

Most of the organizations in the United States today that claim the professional mantle of deradicalization or support for formers (including Light Upon Light/Parallel Networks, Life After Hate, Christian Picciolini's recently disbanded Free Radicals Project, Jeff Schoep's Beyond Barriers, Parents for Peace, and Hands of Eir) rely heavily on "formers" and are wholly or partly led by them. There is often a shifting of membership and alliances between deradicalization projects, with splits and tensions between some, sometimes accompanied by lawsuits.

There are, no doubt, some very sincere people involved in many of these organizations, including former fascists who deeply regret the harm they committed in their pasts and are dedicated to helping others leave hate behind. The journeys made by individuals out of hate and violence and into a renewed commitment to human dignity are at times deeply inspiring; one can acknowledge the courage these journeys involve without erasing the responsibility these individuals now carry, without minimizing the harm they committed, and without putting them on pedestals. (There is a tendency in some circles to treat former neo-Nazis as "aging rock stars."[51])

However, not all organizations are equal. For example, there is an emerging consensus among sincere formers that Light Upon Light is problematic. Light Upon Light was co-founded by former Al Qaeda propagandist Jesse Morton and former New York Police Department intelligence analyst Mitch Silber. In 2019, one of the organization's representatives began working closely with Clarion Project.[52] Light Upon Light also picked up and promoted Jeff Schoep, who led the neo-Nazi National Socialist Movement (NSM) for over two decades and very quickly emerged as a spokesperson for Light Upon Light, when he had been out of the NSM for less than a year and was still being sued for his involvement in the Charlottesville, Virginia, hate march. Light Upon Light has also tweeted enthusiastically about meeting with fascist Jason Kessler, among other likely problematic associations (such as its presence at Heritage Foundation and Turning Point USA events). Shortly after bringing Jeff Schoep on board, Light Upon Light recruited Matthew Heimbach, founder of the fascist Traditionalist Workers Party and who is also presenting himself as reformed. However, Heimbach's ideology does not appear to have changed. Heimbach tended to espouse a workerist, "Strasserite" style of fascism; he has long been willing to build a multiracial coalition to support antisemitism and homophobia.[53] In July 2020, after being promoted as deradicalized and speaking on a Light Upon Light panel, he was found posting publicly his admiration of Romanian fascist Corneliu Codreanu, whom he called "a Saint in my book"; praising Holocaust denier David Irving; and suggesting that LGBTQ+ people should be thrown in prison for "degeneracy." In fact, investigation by Shane Burley found that when Matt Heimbach had initially written to Jesse Morton for help, he had written, "I am not apologizing and have nothing to apologize for," yet Jesse

Morton immediately offered to connect Heimbach with the *New York Times* for an interview about leaving white nationalism.[54]

Unfortunately, formers as well as academics and other experts who work closely with them in the deradicalization field rarely explain necessary and substantive internal disagreements in the field to the public, although this may be beginning to change. Typically, denunciations occur via tweet, if at all. (For example, to my knowledge, no one in the "deradicalization establishment," so to speak, ever called a press conference to denounce the activities of Light Upon Light.) It appears that there may be a culture among formers and their close associates in the deradicalization field of covering for one another to the public, in part because formers have all experienced public shame and judgment for their past behavior and understand one another's struggles in a way that outsiders do not and perhaps also because they know in some cases that their full stories have not been told publicly. (One has to wonder about so many unprosecuted crimes in these individuals' pasts and who has been granted some kind of immunity and whether they all feel legally able to talk about some of the things they have done.) One gets the impression that the community of formers is constantly trying to keep up appearances, knowing that some among them are hacks or grifters but not wishing to draw too much public attention to this because they know that this could undermine the public perception of all formers and of the deradicalization work in which they are engaged (to which there are few alternatives that do not involve formers). Despite the presence of many sincere people, including formers, in deradicalization work, the longer abuses and incompetency are allowed to fester in the deradicalization field, the higher the risk that the field will lose all credibility in the long run.

Harms of the Compassion Narrative

Another factor that needs to be considered in the role of formers is the social impact of a rhetorical trope,[55] which I call "the compassion narrative." Many stories are circulating in print, online media, and public lectures, about how unexpected acts of compassion from members of marginalized groups allegedly precipitated the disengagement of neo-Nazis and white supremacists from their movements. For example: (1) Rising young white supremacist activist and son of prominent white supremacist leader Don Black, Derek Black, formed friendships with Jewish students in college. (2) Former neo-Nazi Ken Parker had transformative encounters with Muslim filmmaker Deeyah Khan and shortly after with a Black pastor who reached out to him. (3) Former neo-Nazi Arno Michaelis was gently challenged about his swastika tattoo by a kind African American woman working in a McDonald's restaurant. Derek Black, Ken Parker, and Arno Michaelis all credit these encounters, at least partly, with leading them to exit white supremacist movements. These stories can be inspirational for some (perhaps especially white, liberal, Christian) members of the general public, but they present certain limitations and potential harms as well, in my view.

The compassion narrative stresses the transformative power of receiving compassion from a person who belongs to a group one has dehumanized, when this compassionate response is unpredicted and feels undeserved. When depicted as an event in a former hater's life, the kindness of the other is met with surprise, shame, and cognitive dissonance on the part of the hater, who later reflects on the meaning of receiving kindness from a member of a group they believed to be inferior and against whom they had mobilized fear, hatred, and violence. These encounters sometimes appear in documentary films,[56] as well as in popular books[57] or academic writing, but usually these narratives are recounted after the fact by formers.

As "exit" programs proliferated in Europe, so did the publication of memoirs by former neo-Nazi skinheads, confessing their acts of violence and sharing their stories of personal redemption. This trend has spread to North America[58] with the publication of books by T.J. Leyden (2008),[59] Kerry Noble (2010),[60] Arno Michaelis (2012),[61] Elisa Hategan (2014),[62] Frank Meeink (2017),[63] Christian Picciolini (2017),[64] Tony McAleer (2019),[65] and others.

Now the American and English-speaking public has been the audience of compassion narratives through dozens of media interviews or speeches by former neo-Nazis or far-right extremists, including Arno Michaelis,[66] Christian Picciolini,[67] Angela King,[68] Frank Meeink,[69] Tony McAleer,[70] Ivan Humble, and Brad Galloway,[71] all of whom now or recently have had public roles in disengaging others from hate groups and who have told their stories many times.

The compassion narrative directly or implicitly holds up the actions of members of marginalized groups in doing outreach to white supremacists as a model for others to follow. For example, audiences may be told, after hearing such a story, to "go out and...find someone that you think is undeserving of your compassion and give it to them."[72] The compassion narrative presents itself as both a tactical and a moral model, suggesting that compassion is both the *most practical* means of deradicalizing extremists (e.g., more effective than countering them in a debate) and the *morally preferable* response (as sometimes contrasted with shunning, "shaming," or violence). As a morally preferable response, it is also proffered as a meaningful experience to those engaging in compassionate outreach, leading perhaps to a kind of gaslighting in which vulnerable people placing themselves in danger are also expected to be happy about it. Although the compassion narrative sometimes includes caveats about boundaries or safety, it often does not, and it almost never includes specific articulations or concrete examples of how members of targeted groups (or those otherwise vulnerable) should set boundaries with extremists who wish them harm.

Unclear Function of the Compassion Narrative

It is not entirely clear what function the compassion narrative is intended to serve. In attempting to understand the frequent use of such stories, I often felt, as Liz Fekete writes of her attempts to understand European Exit groups, that I was encountering a peculiar kind of "cult" speaking some kind of "psychobabble."[73] As feel-good stories that attract reliable curious audiences, compassion narratives serve a purpose in publicizing the work of deradicalization groups and funding their efforts through honorariums received. Surely, however, the repeated, patterned use of this trope is more than mere marketing.

The compassion narrative does not seem to be intended primarily as a tool for disengaging people from hate groups (i.e., as a "counter-narrative," although there is at least one study that refers to it loosely in that way[74]), nor is it simply a factual explanation for the public of what generally gets people out of hate groups. Nor does it seem to be simply a tool for formers' personal healing.

There is growing interest in the role of "narratives" in both "radicalization" and "deradicalization." Because narratives (stories) have power to drive violence, some deradicalization research explores the idea of "counter-narratives," on the hypothesis that since narratives play such a role in recruitment and radicalization, narratives may also be the means to counter-recruit or to disengage people from "violent extremism." Although most of the research on narratives and terrorism focuses on ISIS and not on white supremacist groups, conspiracy theory narratives such as "the great replacement," "cultural Marxism," and "white genocide" have inspired white supremacist and far-right terrorism. However, there is still no scientific study demonstrating the effectiveness of "counter-narratives" in disengaging any kind of "extremists" (let alone white supremacists specifically), nor do researchers share a common definition of counter-narratives. In short, aside from the work of a very small number of serious researchers, "counter-narrative" appears to be mainly a buzzword designed to get government grants.

It is possible that compassion narratives are intended to serve as a form of counter-recruitment from the violent far-right, but they seem unlikely to be good tools for this. Some researchers argue that the use of counter-narratives has not been proven effective in combating terrorism of any kind.[75] One of the most famous experiments with "counter-narratives" was widely adjudged a massive failure. The U.S. State Department designed a series of ads against ISIS, called "Think Again, Turn Away," which bore the State Department logo and merely led to online debates and mockery.[76] This led researchers to conclude that counter-narratives need to be perceived as coming from a trustworthy source in order to be effective.[77] Thus, practically the only thing researchers agree on about counter-narratives points to compassion narratives from formers as not being useful. Although people already desiring to leave hate groups might find it rational to contact formers who have already made the same journey, formers are de facto untrustworthy to convinced movement participants, who often view them as traitors, police, or brainwashed pawns of a Jewish conspiracy.

While not likely to be useful as a counter-narrative, the compassion narrative also does not seem to serve as simply a factual explanation of how disengagement from hate groups generally occurs. Compassion is hardly the only factor that can precipitate disengagement from hate groups. Deradicalization experts note a range of "push" and "pull" factors.[78] Many factors, such as incarceration, disillusionment with group leaders or group dynamics, or wanting to raise a family in a safer or healthier environment, can contribute to people leaving movements. Even in cases where compassion from marginalized others is cited by "formers" themselves as having played a major role in their decision to leave the movement, an examination of their biographies will show it was not the only factor. For example, some white supremacists formed friendships with members of marginalized groups in prison after being incarcerated for hate crimes or shortly after leaving prison, and incarceration thus played a role in interrupting their activities and positioning them to encounter the other in a different setting. Becoming unemployable, lacking meaningful community connections, or exhaustion from living a life on the edge—all situations that can be accelerated by antifascist tactics, incidentally—may also put people in the position to seek to leave movements behind. In the case of Derek Black, who was moved to leave the white supremacist movement through his friendship with Jewish students, it was only after a period of ostracization for his views and mass protest by fellow students that Derek Black accepted an offer to join the weekly Shabbat dinners that precipitated his exit from the white supremacist movement;[79] his social isolation indirectly led him to seek out a new way of relating to the world. Even mockery and humiliation have played a role in getting some people to leave hate groups.[80] Among the repeatedly told stories of "formers" influenced by compassion, some are about the power of compassion received after involvement in the white supremacist movement had ended (e.g., Tony McAleer, Timothy Zaal), and some others note other contributing factors in their disengagement from the movement alongside compassion, such as exhaustion (e.g., Arno Michaelis), incarceration (e.g., Angela King, Frank Meeink), and financial difficulties and family responsibilities (e.g., Christian Picciolini[81]).

Since telling one's story can be necessary for healing from trauma[82] as well as taking responsibility, formers likely do need settings in which to safely share their stories. However, the compassion narrative is more than a therapeutic attempt to grapple with one's past—it is projected into the mass media and offered as an explanation and as advice to the public. In fact, the telling of compassion narratives might be counter-productive to the healing of formers, as some have noted.[83] Beyond mere processing of traumatic events, narratives can also compensate for a feeling of powerlessness[84] by explaining aspects of reality that are disturbing and providing "closure." Telling one's own story can make one feel important, powerful, and immortal ("living on" through one's story).[85] Telling one's story even enables one to be a "hero"[86] who has gone on a "hero's journey"[87] and emerged victorious. From the standpoint of former white supremacists, a sense of "closure" may be risky, since healing from involvement in organized hate and overcoming racism is a lifelong endeavor. Furthermore, there may be motivations to tell stories inaccurately in some cases, leaving out important details to protect oneself or former group associates or exaggerating acts of violence or past leadership roles for shock value, attention, or clout. (That the compassion narrative highlights the power of forgiveness, of course, works to the advantage of anyone who does not want hard questions asked about their past—audience members who ask intrusive-seeming questions or demand proof of reform may appear to be undermining the important work of deradicalization by their unforgiving attitude.)

A problematic kind of "closure" may be provided to some hearers as well, as well as feeding societal attitudes of toxic positivity.[88] The suggestion that closure has been achieved once the former white supremacist publicly repents—the prodigal has returned, and all is forgiven—conveys a variety of messages. While the stories may be "feel-good" redemption narratives for some audience members, for some victims and likely targets of hate, these stories are more ambiguous or possibly harmful. One must ask whether these stories give adequate consideration to the experience of victims, and whether they may set up a division among victims, prizing only those who forgive their attackers. One also has to wonder what it is like for a victim of hate crime to see their former victimizer being applauded as reformed on Oprah-style television programs. As a society, we do need to give people an opportunity to change, and I am not of the opinion that formers should be required to keep silent in public, but there seems to be no serious study or evidence-based research on how to tell formers' stories in a way that does not do harm.

Advice as the Main Function of the Compassion Narrative

Ultimately, I believe, the compassion narrative serves chiefly as advice to activists and the general public, advice that can be summed up as *engage in kind outreach to extremists, or get out of the way.* In a CNN television interview following the Islamophobic mass shooting in Christchurch, New Zealand, Frank Meeink suggested "not opening your house and letting your guard down completely, but at least [having] lunch and talking" with a member of a hate group, should one happen to know such a person.[89]

Similarly, Shannon Martinez, another former white supremacist, was asked in an interview: "Not everyone has the expertise or background to take on the kind of work you do, but is there anything an average person can do to confront radicalism?" and urged people in response to "develop compassion and empathy, particularly for viewpoints you might find abhorrent," "listen to the story behind people's stories, and invite opening questions," and "disarm shame by being open, sharing the worst things we've done, and the worst things that have been done to us."[90] What is essentially happening here, with formers, is that (perhaps out a sense of desperation due to the mounting resurgence of fascist movements and lack of resources for disengaging people from them) disengagement advice is being dispensed to the general public in the hopes that individual members of the public will get people out of hate groups. In this case, the public is being urged to open up to extremists about the worst things they have done or experienced. What seems like a private process that might occur in a support and accountability group, something akin to an Alcoholics Anonymous circle, is now being suggested by many formers as a public task. Might this not actually be dangerous? Yet this type of advice is absolutely the norm across dozens of former hate group members involved in the deradicalization space.

The compassion narrative rarely includes cautionary disclaimers about the risks involved in doing outreach to haters, though there are exceptions. Some former white supremacists couple their accounts of compassionate encounters with a disclaimer stating that compassion must be accompanied by "boundaries" or not evade "consequences," although these terms generally are left unexplained. One former offered this disclaimer in a talk:

> We...former violent extremists have the ability to go out and deal with current extremists...in a way that others can't be expected to. I certainly would never ask a person of color to go hug a Nazi or to take that step... We have to be cautious when we advise people to go out and use compassion and use kindness. It changes lives, but be careful how you do it. I can go into dangerous situations...but I wouldn't say that across the board everyone should go hugging neo-Nazis.[91]

Formers sometimes make such disclaimers, but I have never seen anything much more descriptive (after listening to and reading dozens of compassion narratives purveyed to the general public) in articulating the risks of compassionate outreach or how to do it safely. As someone who has done community activist work and public education in response to hate group incidents, I cannot even begin to tell you how many well-meaning and naïve white liberals want to do incredibly dangerous things, like invite a random Nazi over for tea and cookies to "show them compassion" and change them. Many people need to be educated about the real danger that hate groups pose to whole communities.

As a message to activists against hate groups, compassion narratives serve to discourage certain tactics, such as street violence, ostracism of white supremacists, or "doxxing." Activists may be told, for example, that violence, ridicule ("shaming"), social isolation resulting from ostracism or from exclusion from certain spaces, or consequences such as job loss may radicalize white supremacists further and increase their threat to communities. Compassion, it is suggested, is more effective. The compassion narrative, second, also is a message for the general public, for purposes that likely include helping people to understand how and why people are recruited into white supremacist groups (although its answer to this question is not wholly accurate), providing hope by assuring people that individuals do leave these movements, humanizing white supremacists without endorsing their behavior, and encouraging members of the public to engage in acts of compassion as opposed to increased polarization or judgment toward others.

In the following section, I address the three potential harms from the compassion narrative as currently employed that may impact activists and members of targeted groups.

Potential Harms of the Compassion Narrative

The compassion narrative has potential to do harm in a number of respects.

First, when vulnerable individuals choose *not* to do what might be deemed appropriately courageously compassionate in light of the "compassion narrative," they may face a form of victim-blaming (or self-blame), especially if their refusal to engage in "compassionate" action is followed by the increased radicalization of their antagonists. The rational actions of individuals and communities taken to protect themselves can easily be misjudged as dangerous mistakes or even labeled as coldness or "bullying" toward perpetrators. If a school expels a student, a company fires a worker, or a business refuses service to a customer because of that person's advocacy of bigotry or violence, this may be seen as isolating the individual more and making them more prone to "extremism," instead of being understood as boundary-setting that keeps fascist movements from spreading and recruiting, and as making potential targets of fascism safer by reducing their involuntary contact with those who wish them harm.

Furthermore, if compassion narratives are absorbed by those who act to protect others by ostracizing extremists, activists will also experience undue feelings of guilt. Thus, the social consequences of the compassion narrative can cause a ricochet effect, even retraumatizing or revictimizing vulnerable communities. Such victim-blaming has broader social consequences, promoting prejudice by burdening the oppressed with saving their oppressors, as though this job naturally falls to them. This recapitulates problematic social expectations that expect Black people to educate white people about racism in a gentle, non-"threatening" manner; that expect Muslims to prove their patriotism and nonviolence; that expect women to change and transform men through the power of their love; and so on. Instead of being agents of their own liberation, the oppressed become secondary, supporting characters in a morality play centered on the salvation of perpetrators. Thus, vulnerable communities may be (or *feel*) instrumentalized for the purposes of helping extremists. Individuals may be left feeling revictimized, targeted first by extremists and then asked to bear the weight of defending their community through emotional labor and potentially risky outreach, which can feel like simply giving more to those who have already harmed them.

Activists and members of marginalized groups may already be "compassioning" at close to full capacity, doing emotional labor to support traumatized people in their communities and facing down a variety of injustices and threats from without. To them, the message that compassion heals fascists may not be received as a message of hope but may easily come off as:

> *Your community is suffering because you are not "compassioning" hard enough. It is already your fault that you and your community are in danger, and you can only heal and protect yourself and your community by taking on more (physical and emotional) risk.*

This message exacerbates the shame and guilt that tend to accompany activist burnout, the sense that one is not doing "enough" to alleviate suffering.[92]

The compassion narrative may also undermine healthy personal and societal boundaries essential for protecting vulnerable individuals, by encouraging people to take dangerous risks in socializing with those who wish them harm. Because the compassion narrative rarely includes any concrete advice beyond that of showing compassion carefully, it leaves communities with two options: passively submitting to the authority of those they may be told are "experts" (such as former fascists or law enforcement and the academics and think tank employees in those circles) for ongoing guidance, or deciding on their own, based in part on a confusing narrative, how to show "compassion" while also taking account of their safety. If they choose to submit to experts, they cede power in a situation where they are already experiencing a loss of power, in exchange for the hope of safety. If they respond to undue pressure or inaccurate information about the power of compassion, they may be further endangered or harmed. It is better, in my opinion, for communities to make their own informed judgments and not to discount their own expertise and to take outsiders who tell them what their boundaries should be with a grain of salt.

Finally, compassion narratives are easily co-opted by the far-right, just as the far-right also co-opts the language of "extremism." For the far-right, the compassion narrative can be used to criticize activism against hate as shutting down necessary dialogue and can be used to defend problematic alliances.

Consider, for example, an article in "intellectual dark web"[93] magazine *Quillette* responding to revelations that poet Frank Sherlock had been in a white supremacist band in the 1980s. While offering no explanation of Sherlock's personal history or the movement he was part of, the author of the article surmises that by admitting to have been in a white supremacist band, Sherlock may have wanted to use his past to educate, like formers, and cites Christian Picciolini and Frank Meeink as examples. The life stories of formers are weaponized here, to snuff out immediately the inevitable demands for information and accountability on the part of a notable poet who had only just been revealed to have been engaged in the white supremacist movement. The author continues:

> Maybe Sherlock thought his admission might be a teachable moment for others—to provide hope, especially to those alienated teenagers who were just like he was and who might likewise be susceptible to indoctrination. He might have even hoped to be commended for denouncing his stained past and correcting course, and maybe even given a little sympathy, compassion, and understanding. But that was too much to ask of the internet.[94]

In raising these concerns about compassion narratives, I do not wish to police the decisions of impacted individuals or communities about the level of risk they are willing to accept. It is the "policing" nature of the compassion narrative, in fact, that is problematic. My point here is also not that compassionate outreach is always ineffective at disengaging extremists—in general, if one's goal is to reach people, compassion is more likely to get through to them than meanness (although this is so commonsense that it could almost only come as a profound revelation to someone who had spent years hardening themselves for race war and shutting down their basic empathic instincts). Although I do not do work "disengaging" people from hate groups, I myself have engaged in compassionate outreach to a smattering of people both on the brink of being drawn into the far-right and to people who have recently left it behind, and I do not regret those decisions at all. Rather, I am concerned with a discourse that seems to place peculiar burdens on others for reasons that are unclear. The burden of proof lies on those who frequently use compassion narratives to show that these narratives do more good than harm and to ensure that, if these narratives are shared, the public is receiving accurate information and not being manipulated.

Transcending the Counter-Extremism Model

Surmounting the limitations of the "counter-extremism" model of analysis with regard to fascism will continue to be difficult for those who rely on government grants and close relationships with law enforcement agencies. Some collaboration among researchers and advocates against hate remains possible across differing worldviews and discourses. The urgency of the present moment would make refusing to work together with some potential allies based on ideological differences foolish. However, critiquing the limitations of extremism and radicalization models is necessary for left praxis in opposing fascism.

Much can be done to transcend the extremism model. More fruitful collaboration with Muslims fighting Islamophobia could be developed, and learning from their critiques could be valuable; closer relationships with Muslim civil rights groups would be a good sign of progress in centrist work against hate. The U.S. left can help foster a stronger analysis and praxis by exploring the interconnections between U.S. imperialism and white supremacy and settler colonialism at home. Dissenting academics and formers who are critical of internal problems in the field can continue to speak out and build alliances that allow them to do work helping people leave hate groups or preventing violence, without perpetuating problematic narratives that lead to alliances with hate groups or to victim-blaming.

Ultimately, overcoming the limitations of the counter-extremism model requires challenging the core assumption that fascists are extremists "over there"—something weird to gawk at for entertainment—unlike moderate, clean centers of power. It requires looking at structural racism, intersecting oppressions, authoritarian policies, and capitalism's failure to accord a decent standard of living and dignity for all and seeing how these structures and systems give rise to fascism as a movement and a political possibility. In short, it requires understanding fascism not only as a psychological or a criminological problem but also as a social movement seeking power, always already connected to sources of power. As I have already argued, this does not mean that empathy for fascists or an understanding of the psychological appeal of fascism for those who join fascist movements is inherently reactionary (right-wing). It simply means that theorizing fascism as fringe extremism and failing to critically analyze social structures will impoverish our practice and limit our solidarity.

Notes

1 Liz Fekete, *Europe's Fault Lines: Racism and the Rise of the Right* (London: Verso, 2019), 31–2.
2 Sara Diamond, *Roads to Dominion: Right-wing Movements and Political Power in the United States* (New York: Guilford Press, 1995), 5.
3 Fekete, *Europe's Fault Lines*, 131–3.
4 Fekete, *Europe's Fault Lines*, 160.
5 Aurelien Mondon and Aaron Winter, *Reactionary Democracy: How Racism and the Populist Far-Right Became Mainstream* (London: Verso, 2020), 60.

6 Kay Whitlock and Michael Bronski, *Considering Hate: Violence, Goodness, and Justice in American Culture and Politics* (Boston, MA: Beacon Press, 2015), 74.

7 Department of Justice, "Attorney General William P. Barr's Statement on Riots and Domestic Terrorism," May 31, 2020, accessed July 3, 2020, https://www.justice.gov/opa/pr/attorney-general-william-p-barrs-statement-riots-and-domestic-terrorism.

8 Matt Zapotosky, "Barr Forms Task Force to Counter Anti-Government Extremists," *Washington Post*, June 26, 2020, https://www.washingtonpost.com/national-security/william-barr-task-force-anti-government-extremists-antifa-boogaloo/2020/06/26/138f424e-b7bf-11ea-a510-55bf26485c93_story.html.

9 Alexander Reid Ross, *Against the Fascist Creep* (Chico: AK Press, 2017).

10 Wolfgang Wippermann, "Politologentrug: Ideologiekritik der Extremismus-Legende," *Standpunkte*, October 2010, https://www.rosalux.de/fileadmin/rls_uploads/pdfs/Standpunkte/Standpunkte_10-2010.pdf.

11 Wolfgang Wippermann, "Politologentrug: Ideologiekritik der Extremismus-Legende," *Standpunkte*, October 2010, https://www.rosalux.de/fileadmin/rls_uploads/pdfs/Standpunkte/Standpunkte_10-2010.pdf.

12 Chip Berlet and Matthew N. Lyons, "Repression and Ideology: The Legacy of Discredited Centrist/Extremist Theory," *Political Research Associates*, November 17, 1998, https://politicalresearch.org/sites/default/files/2018-10/repression.pdf.

13 Berlet and Lyons, "Repression and Ideology."

14 Berlet and Lyons, "Repression and Ideology."

15 Berlet and Lyons, "Repression and Ideology."

16 Berlet and Lyons, "Repression and Ideology."

17 Berlet and Lyons, "Repression and Ideology," 17.

18 Jack Buckby, *Monster of Their Own Making: How the Far Left, the Media, and Politicians are Creating Far-Right Extremists* (New York: Bombardier Books, 2020), 10.

19 Office for the Protection of the Constitution, "Fields of Work," July 3, 2020, https://www.verfassungsschutz.de/en/fields-of-work.

20 William T. Cavanaugh, *The Myth of Religious Violence: Secular Ideology and the Roots of Modern Conflict* (Oxford: Oxford University Press, 2009), 4.

21 Roger Eatwell, "Community Cohesion and Cumulative Extremism in Contemporary Britain," *The Political Quarterly* 77, no. 2 (April–June 2006): 204–16.

22 Bridge Initiative Team, "Factsheet: Maajid Nawaz," December 4, 2018, accessed July 4, 2020, https://bridge.georgetown.edu/research/factsheet-maajid-nawaz-2/.

23 Southern Poverty Law Center, "Anti-Muslim," July 2, 2020, https://www.splcenter.org/fighting-hate/extremist-files/ideology/anti-muslim.

24 Shireen Qudosi, "Opinion: The Movement to Destroy a Nation," *Clarion Project*, June 24, 2020, accessed July 2, 2020, https://clarionproject.org/the-movement-to-destroy-a-nation/.

25 Southern Poverty Law Center, "Hate Map," accessed July 2, 2020, https://www.splcenter.org/hate-map.

26 Arun Kundnani, "Radicalisation: Journey of a Concept," *Race & Class* 54, no. 2 (2012): 7.

27 Lisa Stampnitzsky, *Disciplining Terror: How "Experts" Invented Terrorism* (Cambridge: Cambridge University Press, 2013), 188–9.

28 Angela Davis, *Are Prisons Obsolete?* (New York: Seven Stories Press, 2003).

29 Suhaiymah Manzoor-Khan, *Tangled in Terror: Uprooting Islamophobia* (London: Pluto Press, 2022), 62–77.

Tarek Younis, "Counter-Radicalization: A Critical Look into a Racist New Industry." *Yaqeen Institute*, 2019, https://yaqeeninstitute.org/read/paper/counter-radicalization-a-critical-look-into-a-racist-new-industry. Tarek Younis, *The Muslim, State and Mind: Psychology in Times of Islamophobia* (London, SAGE: 2024).

30 Rob Faure Walker, *The Emergence of "Extremism": Exposing the Violent Discourse and Language of "Radicalization"* (London: Bloomsbury, 2022), 7–11.

31 Simon Wiesenthal Center (@simonwiesenthal), "Necessary Move," May 31, 2020, https://twitter.com/simonwiesenthal/status/1267159665164513281.

32 Wendy Brown, *Regulating Aversion: Tolerance in the Age of Identity and Empire* (Princeton, NJ: Princeton University Press, 2006), 107.

33 Brown, 109.

34 Brown, 124.

35 Allison Weir, "Israeli Organ Harvesting," *Counterpunch*, August 28, 2009, accessed June 30, 2020, https://www.counterpunch.org/2009/08/28/israeli-organ-harvesting/.

36 William Echikson, "Viktor Órban's Antisemitism Problem," *Politico*, May 13, 2019, https://www.politico.eu/article/viktor-orban-anti-semitism-problem-hungary-jews/; DW, "New School Curriculum Raises Eyebrows in Orban's Hungary," accessed May 23, 2021, https://www.dw.com/en/new-school-curriculum-raises-eyebrows-in-orbans-hungary/a-52964617.

37 Nadine Naber and Junaid Rana, "The 21st Century Problem of Anti-Muslim Racism," *Jadaliyya*, July 25, 2019, accessed August 8, 2020, https://www.jadaliyya.com/Details/39830?fbclid=IwAR3GbEyRv95eu5Qf7dTXem3MiyeyKOWH8vw_6e3ny0O9FA2CEJ_2qNeIBEM.

38 Christopher J. Morris, "Can Partnership Approaches Developed to Prevent Islamic Terrorism Be Replicated for the Extreme Right? Comparing the Muslim Brotherhood and Generation Identity as 'Firewalls' Against Violent Extremism," *Journal for Deradicalization* (2021): 34–79.

39 Muslim Justice League, "Statement: AMEMSA Groups Oppose Expansion of the Countering Violent Extremism Program," accessed October 27, 2019, https://www.muslimjusticeleague.org/wp-content/uploads/2017/09/Statement-AMEMSA-Groups-Oppose-Expansion-of-the-Countering-Violent-Extremism-Program.pdf. Unicorn Riot, "Twin Cities Young Muslim Collective Holds CVE Forum," November 9, 2016, https://unicornriot.ninja/2016/twin-cities-young-muslim-collective-holds-cve-forum/. Debbie Southorn, "We Can't Fight Trump-Style Hate with the Surveillance State," *In These Times*, September 19, 2017, accessed October 27, 2019. http://inthesetimes.com/article/20531/CVE-surveillance-donald-trump-life-after-hate-islamophobia. Vanessa Taylor, "2020 Candidates Want to Fund a Program Used to Surveil Muslims on Social Media," *Vice*, October 17, 2019, accessed October 27, 2019, https://www.vice.com/en_us/article/xwemzd/2020-candidates-want-to-fund-a-program-used-to-surveil-muslims-on-social-media.

40 Brennan Center for Justice. "Why Countering Violent Extremism Programs are Bad Policy," *Brennan Center for Justice*, September 9, 2019, https://www.brennancenter.org/our-work/research-reports/why-countering-violent-extremism-programs-are-bad-policy.

41 Arun Kundnani, *The Muslims Are Coming!: Islamophobia, Extremism, and the Domestic War on Terror* (New York: Verso, 2015).

42 Waqas Mirza, "Denver's Counter-Terror Program Sets Sights on Black Lives Matter, LGBT Groups, and Refugees," *Muckrock*, March 9, 2017, accessed October 27, 2019, https://www.muckrock.com/news/archives/2017/mar/09/denvers-counterterror-BLM/.

43 Nicole Nguyen, *Suspect Communities: Anti-Muslim Racism and the Domestic War on Terror* (Minneapolis: University of Minnesota Press, 2019); Nicole Nguyen and Yazan Zahzah, *Why Treating White Supremacy as Domestic Terrorism Won't Work and How Not to Fall for It: A Toolkit for Social Justice Advocates*.

44 Liz Fekete, "Exit from White Supremacism: The Accountability Gap Within Europe's De-Radicalisation Programs." *Institute of Race Relations: Briefing*, September 2014.

45 James Allsup, "Speech, American Renaissance," *YouTube* (no longer online).

46 Picciolini, *Breaking Hate*, 109.

47 Picciolini, *Breaking Hate*, 165.

48 Christian Picciolini, "I Have Found that Most 'Deradicalization" Orgs Are Simply Right-Wing Grant Mills. I Trust None of Them," May 17, 2022, https://twitter.com/cpicciolini/status/1526596787754176514.

49 For example, some have raised this concern about Jeff Schoep. See, for example, Southern Poverty Law Center, "Jeff Schoep," accessed November 20, 2021, https://www.splcenter.org/fighting-hate/extremist-files/individual/jeff-schoep.

50 Liz Fekete, "Exit from White Supremacism: The Accountability Gap Within Europe's De-radicalisation Programmes," Institute of Race Relations, September 2014.

51 Fekete, *Europe's Fault Lines*, 147.

52 Clarion Project, "Former Extremists Frank Meeink and Tanya Joya: The Way Back".

53 Brett Barrouquere, "Two Prominent Neo-Nazis Recant, But Their Actions Sow Doubts," *Southern Poverty Law Center*, May 14, 2020, https://www.splcenter.org/hatewatch/2020/05/14/two-prominent-neo-nazis-recant-their-actions-sow-doubts.

54 Shane Burley, "Can You Ever Trust a Former White Nationalist?", *The Public Eye*, Winter 2022, https://politicalresearch.org/2022/05/11/can-you-ever-trust-former-white-nationalist.

55 Sveinung Sandberg, "The Importance of Stories Untold: Life-Story, Event Story, and Trope," *Crime, Media, Culture* 12, no. 2 (2016): 153–71.

56 *White Right: Meeting the Enemy*, directed by Deeyah Khan (Fuuse, 2017); *Accidental Courtesy: Daryl Davis, Race & America*, directed by Matthew Ornstein (2016); Frankie Meeink, "First Ever Show of a Former Racist Doing an Intervention on a Current Racist AMAZING!", October 2017, accessed August 18, 2019, https://www.youtube.com/watch?v=DTvowOVGQRo; Christian Picciolini, *Breaking Hate*, MSNBC.

57 Eli Saslow, *Rising Out of Hatred: The Awakening of a Former White Nationalist* (Doubleday, 2018).

58 Fekete, "Exit from White Supremacism."

59 T.J. Leyden and Bridget M. Cook, *Skinhead Confessions: From Hate to Hope* (Springville, UT: Sweetwater Books, 2008).

60 Kerry Noble, *Tabernacle of Hate: Seduction into Right-wing Extremism* (Syracuse: Syracuse University Press, 2010).

61 Arno Michaelis, *My Life After Hate* (Milwaukee: Authentic Presence, 2012).

62 Elisa Hategan, *Race Traitor: The True Story of Canadian Intelligence's Greatest Cover-up* (Toronto: Incognito Press, 2014).

63 Frank Meeink and Jody Roy, *Autobiography of a Recovering Skinhead: The Frank Meeink Story as Told to Jody M. Roy*, et al. (Portland: Hawthorne Books, 2017).

64 Christian Picciolini, *White American Youth: My Descent into America's Most Violent Hate Movement—And How I Got Out* (New York: Hachette Books, 2017).

65 Tony McAleer, *The Cure for Hate: A Former White Supremacist's Journey from Violent Extremism to Radical Compassion* (Vancouver, BC: Arsenal Pulp Press, 2019).

66 Arno Michaelis, "Essay: Dear Nice Old Black Lady at the McDonald's," *WUWM*, January 3, 2018, accessed August 19, 2019. https://www.wuwm.com/post/essay-dear-nice-old-black-lady-mcdonalds#stream/0.

67 Picciolini, *White American Youth*.

68 Claire Bates, "I Was a Neo-Nazi: Then I Fell in Love With a Black Woman," *BBC*, August 29, 2017, accessed August 20, 2019, https://www.bbc.com/news/magazine-40779377.

69 Michael Kimmel, 126, 128–9.
70 How-To Heretic Podcast, "The Other Ark," https://howtoheretic.com/podcast/tag/Tony+McAleer.
71 https://www.facebook.com/watch/live/?v=262715745043584&ref=external.
72 Christian Picciolini, "My Descent into America's Neo-Nazi Movement & How I Got Out," *TEDx Talks*, December 20, 2017, https://www.youtube.com/watch?v=SSH5EY-W5oM.
73 Fekete, *Europe's Fault Lines*, 147.
74 Tanya Silverman and Christopher J. Stewart, et al., "The Impact of Counter-Narratives," *Institute for Strategic Dialogue*, https://www.isdglobal.org/wp-content/uploads/2016/08/Impact-of-Counter-Narratives_ONLINE_1.pdf.
75 Eric Rosand and Emily Winterbotham, "Do Counter-Narratives Actually Reduce Violent Extremism?", *Brookings*, March 20, 2019, accessed July 29, 2019, https://www.brookings.edu/blog/order-from-chaos/2019/03/20/do-counter-narratives-actually-reduce-violent-extremism/. Andrew Glazzard, "Losing the Plot: Narrative, Counter-Narrative and Violent Extremism," *International Centre for Counter-Terrorism – The Hague*, May 2017, https://icct.nl/app/uploads/2017/05/ICCT-Glazzard-Losing-the-Plot-May-2017.pdf.
76 Kurt Braddock, *Weaponized Words: The Strategic Role of Persuasion in Violent Radicalization and Counter-Radicalization* (Cambridge: Cambridge University Press, 2020), 6.
77 Kurt Braddock and John F. Morrison, "Cultivating Trust and Perceptions of Source Credibility in Online Counternarratives Intended to Reduce Support for Terrorism", *Studies in Conflict and Terrorism* 43, no. 6 (March 2018):1–50.
78 Daniel Koehler, *Understanding Deradicalization: Methods, Tools, and Programs for Countering Violent Extremism* (London: Routledge, 2017).
79 Saslow, 72.
80 Anders Anglesey, "Tommy Robinson's Uncle Reveals Women 'Spitting in His Face' Made Him Leave Far-Right Group," *Daily Star*, accessed august 15, 2019, https://www.dailystar.co.uk/news/latest-news/tommy-robinson-edl-luton-far-18873575.
81 *White American Youth*.
82 Bessel van der Kolk, *The Body Keeps the Score: Brain, Mind, and Body in the Healing of Trauma* (Penguin: New York, 2014).
83 Life After Hate, "When Former Extremists Go Public: What is the Risk As Our Appetite Grows for New Stories?", *Life After Hate*, February 24, 2020, https://www.lifeafterhate.org/blog/2020/2/14/when-former-extremists-go-public-what-are-the-risks-as-our-appetite-grows-for-new-stories.
84 Lois Presser, *Inside Story: How Narratives Drive Mass Harm* (Oakland: University of California Press, 2018), 83.
85 Lois Presser, *Inside Story*, 83.
86 Lois Presser, *Inside Story*, 82.
87 Life After Hate, "When Former Extremists Go Public: What is the Risk As Our Appetite Grows for New Stories?", *Life After Hate*, February 24, 2020, https://www.lifeafterhate.org/blog/2020/2/14/when-former-extremists-go-public-what-are-the-risks-as-our-appetite-grows-for-new-stories (quoting Pete Simi).
88 Elisa Hategan, "Profiting from Hate: 'Motivational Speakers' Compete Over Who Has the Best Sob Story," *Now Toronto*, December 12, 2019, https://nowtoronto.com/news/hate-neo-nazi-racism-profiteers.
89 CNN, "Why a Former Hate Group Member Started to Think Differently," March 16, 2019, https://www.youtube.com/watch?v=CpqM3H4CJvc.
90 Jane C. Hu, "To De-Radicalize Extremists, Former Neo-Nazis Use a Radical Method: Empathy," *Quartz*, November 9, 2018, accessed October 25, 2019, https://qz.com/1457014/to-deradicalize-extremists-former-neo-nazis-use-a-radical-method-empathy/.

91 "Untold Stories of 'Formers' & the Human Impact," *USC Price*, October 27, 2019, https://www.youtube.com/watch?v=RkqXbIk0iJQ.
92 Laura van Dernoot Lipsky, *The Age of Overwhelm: Strategies for the Long Haul* (Oakland, CA: Berrett-Koehler, 2018).
93 Amelia Lester, "The Voice of the Intellectual 'Dark Web,'" *Politico,* November/December 2018, https://www.politico.com/magazine/story/2018/11/11/intellectual-dark-web-quillette-claire-lehmann-221917.
94 Clint Margrave, "The Impassable Road to Redemption," *Quillette*, April 2019 latest (original version) https://quillette.com/2019/04/24/the-impassable-road-to-redemption/.

Bibliography

Allsup, James. *Talk at American Renaissance* (no longer online).
Anglesey, Anders. "Tommy Robinson's Uncle Reveals Women 'Spitting in His Face' Made Him Leave Far-Right Group," *Daily Star*, August 15, 2019. https://www.dailystar.co.uk/news/latest-news/tommy-robinson-edl-luton-far-18873575.
Barrouquere, Brett. "Two Prominent Neo-Nazis Recant, But Their Actions Sow Doubts." *Southern Poverty Law Center*, May 14, 2020. https://www.splcenter.org/hatewatch/2020/05/14/two-prominent-neo-nazis-recant-their-actions-sow-doubts.
Bates, Claire. "I was a Neo-Nazi: Then I Fell in Love With a Black Woman." *BBC*, August 29, 2017, August 20, 2019. https://www.bbc.com/news/magazine-40779377.
Berlet, Chip and Matthew N. Lyons. "Repression and Ideology: The Legacy of Discredited Centrist/Extremist Theory." *Political Research Associates*, November 17, 1998. https://politicalresearch.org/sites/default/files/2018-10/repression.pdf.
Braddock, Kurt and John F. Morrison. "Cultivating Trust and Perceptions of Source Credibility in Online Counternarratives Intended to Reduce Support for Terrorism." *Studies in Conflict and Terrorism* 43, no. 6 (March 2018): 1–50.
Braddock, Kurt. *Weaponized Words: The Strategic Role of Persuasion in Violent Radicalization and Counter-Radicalization*. Cambridge: Cambridge University Press, 2020.
Brennan Center for Justice. "Why Countering Violent Extremism Programs are Bad Policy." *Brennan Center for Justice*, September 9, 2019. https://www.brennancenter.org/our-work/research-reports/why-countering-violent-extremism-programs-are-bad-policy.
Bridge Initiative Team. "Factsheet: Maajid Nawaz." 2018, July 4, 2020. https://bridge.georgetown.edu/research/factsheet-maajid-nawaz-2/.
Brown, Wendy. *Regulating Aversion: Tolerance in the Age of Identity and Empire*. Princeton, NJ: Princeton University Press, 2006.
Buckby, Jack. *Monster of Their Own Making: How the Far Left, the Media, and Politicians are Creating Far-Right Extremists*. New York: Bombardier Books, 2020.
Burley, Shane. "Can You Ever Trust a Former White Nationalist?" *The Public Eye*. Winter 2022. https://politicalresearch.org/2022/05/11/can-you-ever-trust-former-white-nationalist.
Cavanaugh, William T. *The Myth of Religious Violence: Secular Ideology and the Roots of Modern Conflict*. Oxford: Oxford University Press, 2009.
Clarion Project. "Former Extremists Frank Meeink and Tanya Joya: The Way Back."
CNN. "Why a Former Hate Group Member Started to Think Differently." March 16, 2019. https://www.youtube.com/watch?v=CpqM3H4CJvc.

Davis, Angela. *Are Prisons Obsolete?* New York: Seven Stories Press, 2003.

Department of Justice. "Attorney General William P. Barr's Statement on Riots and Domestic Terrorism." May 31, 2020, July 3, 2020. https://www.justice.gov/opa/pr/attorney-general-william-p-barrs-statement-riots-and-domestic-terrorism.

Diamond, Sara. *Roads to Dominion: Right-wing Movements and Political Power in the United States.* New York: Guilford Press, 1995.

DW. "New School Curriculum Raises Eyebrows in Orban's Hungary." *DW*, May 23, 2021. https://www.dw.com/en/new-school-curriculum-raises-eyebrows-in-orbans-hungary/a-52964617.

Eatwell, Roger. "Community Cohesion and Cumulative Extremism in Contemporary Britain." *The Political Quarterly* 77, no. 2 (April–June 2006): 204–16.

Echikson, William. "Viktor Órban's Antisemitism Problem." *Politico*, May 13, 2019. https://www.politico.eu/article/viktor-orban-anti-semitism-problem-hungary-jews/.

Fekete, Liz. *Europe's Fault Lines: Racism and the Rise of the Right.* London: Verso, 2019.

Fekete, Liz. "Exit from White Supremacism: The Accountability Gap Within Europe's De-Radicalisation Programs." *Institute of Race Relations: Briefing*, September 2014.

Glazzard, Andrew. "Losing the Plot: Narrative, Counter-Narrative and Violent Extremism." *International Centre for Counter-Terrorism – The Hague*, May 2017. https://icct.nl/app/uploads/2017/05/ICCT-Glazzard-Losing-the-Plot-May-2017.pdf.

Harris, Sam and Maajid Nawaz. *Islam and the Future of Tolerance: A Dialogue.* Cambridge, MA: Harvard University Press, 2015.

Hategan, Elisa. "Profiting from Hate: 'Motivational Speakers' Compete Over Who Has the Best Sob Story." *Now Toronto*, December 12, 2019. https://nowtoronto.com/news/hate-neo-nazi-racism-profiteers.

Hategan, Elisa. *Race Traitor: The True Story of Canadian Intelligence's Greatest Cover-up.* Toronto: Incognito Press, 2014.

Hu, Jane C. "To De-Radicalize Extremists, Former Neo-Nazis Use a Radical Method: Empathy." *Quartz.* November 9, 2018. October 25, 2019. https://qz.com/1457014/to-deradicalize-extremists-former-neo-nazis-use-a-radical-method-empathy/.

Kelley, Megan and J. DeCook. "Not So Reformed: How 'Countering Violent Extremism' Groups Elevate 'Former' White Nationalists." *Political Research Associates*, April 1, 2022. https://politicalresearch.org/2022/04/01/not-so-reformed.

Khan, Deeyah. *White Right: Meeting the Enemy*, directed by Deeyah Khan. Fuuse, 2017.

Koehler, Daniel. *Understanding Deradicalization: Methods, Tools, and Programs for Countering Violent Extremism.* London: Routledge, 2017.

Kundnani, Arun. *The Muslims Are Coming!: Islamophobia, Extremism, and the Domestic War on Terror.* New York: Verso, 2015.

Kundnani, Arun. "Radicalisation: Journey of a Concept." *Race & Class* 54, no. 2 (2012): 3–25.

Lester, Amelia. "The Voice of the Intellectual 'Dark Web.'" *Politico*, November/December 2018. https://www.politico.com/magazine/story/2018/11/11/intellectual-dark-web-quillette-claire-lehmann-221917.

Leyden, T.J. and Bridget M. Cook. *Skinhead Confessions: From Hate to Hope.* Springville, UT: Sweetwater Books, 2008.

Life After Hate. "When Former Extremists Go Public: What is the Risk As Our Appetite Grows for New Stories?". *Life After Hate*, February 24, 2020. https://www.lifeafterhate.org/blog/2020/2/14/when-former-extremists-go-public-what-are-the-risks-as-our-appetite-grows-for-new-stories.

Lipsky, Laura van Dernoot. *The Age of Overwhelm: Strategies for the Long Haul.* Oakland, CA: Berrett-Koehler, 2018.

Manzoor-Kahn, Suhaiymah. *Tangled in Terror: Uprooting Islamophobia.* London: Pluto Press, 2022.

Margrave, Clint. "The Impassable Road to Redemption." *Quillette.* April 2019 latest (original version) https://quillette.com/2019/04/24/the-impassable-road-to-redemption/.

McAleer, Tony. *The Cure for Hate: A Former White Supremacist's Journey from Violent Extremism to Radical Compassion.* Vancouver, BC: Arsenal Pulp Press, 2019.

Meeink, Frank and Jody Roy. *Autobiography of a Recovering Skinhead: The Frank Meeink Story as Told to Jody M. Roy, et al.* Portland: Hawthorne Books, 2017.

Meeink, Frankie. "First Ever Show of a Former Racist Doing an Intervention on a Current Racist AMAZING!" October 2017, accessed August 18, 2019. https://www.youtube.com/watch?v=DTvowOVGQRo.

Michaelis, Arno. "Essay: Dear Nice Old Black Lady at the McDonald's." *WUWM,* January 3, 2018, Accessed August 19, 2019. https://www.wuwm.com/post/essay-dear-nice-old-black-lady-mcdonalds#stream/0.

Michaelis, Arno. *My Life After Hate.* Milwaukee: Authentic Presence, 2012.

Mirza, Waqas. "Denver's Counter-Terror Program Sets Sights on Black Lives Matter, LGBT Groups, and Refugees." *Muckrock,* March 9, 2017, Accessed October 27, 2019. https://www.muckrock.com/news/archives/2017/mar/09/denvers-counterterror-BLM/.

Mondon, Aurelien, and Aaron Winter. *Reactionary Democracy: How Racism and the Populist Far-Right Became Mainstream.* London: Verso, 2020.

Morris, Christopher J. "Can Partnership Approaches Developed to Prevent Islamic Terrorism Be Replicated for the Extreme Right? Comparing the Muslim Brotherhood and Generation Identity as 'Firewalls' Against Violent Extremism," *Journal for Deradicalization* 26(2021): 34–79.

Muslim Justice League. "Statement: AMEMSA Groups Oppose Expansion of the Countering Violent Extremism Program." October 27, 2019. https://www.muslimjusticeleague.org/wp-content/uploads/2017/09/Statement-AMEMSA-Groups-Oppose-Expansion-of-the-Countering-Violent-Extremism-Program.pdf.

Naber, Nadine and Junaid Rana. "The 21st Century Problem of Anti-Muslim Racism." *Jadaliyya,* July 25, 2019, Accessed August 8, 2020. https://www.jadaliyya.com/Details/39830?fbclid=IwAR3GbEyRv95eu5Qf7dTXem3MiyeyKOWH8vw_6e3ny0O9FA2CEJ_2qNeIBEM.

Nguyen, Nicole. *Suspect Communities: Anti-Muslim Racism and the Domestic War on Terror.* Minneapolis: University of Minnesota Press, 2019.

Nguyen, Nicole and Yazan Zahzah. *Why Treating White Supremacy as Domestic Terrorism Won't Work and How Not to Fall for It: A Toolkit for Social Justice Advocates.* Stop CVE. October 3, 2023. http://www.stopcve.com/uploads/1/1/2/4/112447985/white_supremacy_toolkit.pdf

Noble, Kerry. *Tabernacle of Hate: Seduction into Right-wing Extremism.* Syracuse: Syracuse University Press, 2010.

Office for the Protection of the Constitution. "Fields of Work." July 3, 2020. https://www.verfassungsschutz.de/en/fields-of-work.

Ornstein, Matthew. *Accidental Courtesy: Daryl Davis, Race & America*, directed by Matthew Ornstein (2016).

Picciolini, Christian. *Breaking Hate: Confronting the New Culture of Extremism.* New York: Hachette, 2020.

Picciolini, Christian. "I Have Found that Most 'Deradicalization' Orgs Are Simply Right-Wing Grant Mills. I Trust None of Them." May 17, 2022. https://twitter.com/cpicciolini/status/1526596787754176514.

Picciolini, Christian. "My Descent into America's Neo-Nazi Movement & How I Got Out." *TEDx Talks*, December 20, 2017. https://www.youtube.com/watch?v=SSH5EY-W5oM.

Picciolini, Christian. *White American Youth: My Descent into America's Most Violent Hate Movement—And How I Got Out.* New York: Hachette Books, 2017.

Presser, Lois. *Inside Story: How Narratives Drive Mass Harm.* Oakland: University of California Press, 2018.

Qudosi, Shireen. "Opinion: The Movement to Destroy a Nation." *Clarion Project*, June 24, 2020, accessed July 2, 2020. https://clarionproject.org/the-movement-to-destroy-a-nation/.

Rosand, Eric and Emily Winterbotham. "Do Counter-Narratives Actually Reduce Violent Extremism?". *Brookings,* March 20, 2019, Accessed July 29, 2019. https://www.brookings.edu/blog/order-from-chaos/2019/03/20/do-counter-narratives-actually-reduce-violent-extremism/.

Ross, Alexander Reid. *Against the Fascist Creep.* Chico: AK Press, 2017.

Sandberg, Sveinung. "The Importance of Stories Untold: Life-Story, Event Story, and Trope." *Crime, Media, Culture* 12, no. 2 (2016): 153–71.

Saslow, Eli. *Rising Out of Hatred: The Awakening of a Former White Nationalist.* New York: Doubleday, 2018.

Silverman, Tanya and Christopher J. Stewart, et al., "The Impact of Counter-Narratives." *Institute for Strategic Dialogue.* https://www.isdglobal.org/wp-content/uploads/2016/08/Impact-of-Counter-Narratives_ONLINE_1.pdf.

Simon Wiesenthal Center (@simonwiesenthal). "Necessary move." May 31, 2020. https://twitter.com/simonwiesenthal/status/1267159665164513281.

Southern Poverty Law Center. "Jeff Schoep." November 20, 2021. https://www.splcenter.org/fighting-hate/extremist-files/individual/jeff-schoep.

Southern Poverty Law Center. "Hate Map." July 2, 2020. https://www.splcenter.org/hate-map.

Southorn, Debbie. "We Can't Fight Trump-Style Hate with the Surveillance State." *In These Times.* September 19, 2017. http://inthesetimes.com/article/20531/CVE-surveillance-donald-trump-life-after-hate-islamophobia.

Stampnitzsky, Lisa. *Disciplining Terror: How "Experts" Invented Terrorism.* Cambridge: Cambridge University Press, 2013.

Taylor, Vanessa. "2020 Candidates Want to Fund a Program Used to Surveil Muslims on Social Media." *Vice*, October 17, 2019, accessed October 27, 2019. https://www.vice.com/en_us/article/xwemzd/2020-candidates-want-to-fund-a-program-used-to-surveil-muslims-on-social-media.

Unicorn Riot. "Twin Cities Young Muslim Collective Holds CVE Forum." November 9, 2016. https://unicornriot.ninja/2016/twin-cities-young-muslim-collective-holds-cve-forum/.

USC Price. "Untold Stories of 'Formers' & the Human Impact." *USC Price*. October 27, 2019. https://www.youtube.com/watch?v=RkqXbIk0iJQ.

Van der Kolk, Bessel. *The Body Keeps the Score: Brain, Mind, and Body in the Healing of Trauma*. Penguin: New York, 2014.

Walker, Rob Faure. *The Emergence of "Extremism": Exposing the Violent Discourse and Language of "Radicalization"*. London: Bloomsbury, 2022.

Weir, Allison. "Israeli Organ Harvesting." *Counterpunch*. August 28, 2009, accessed June 30, 2020. https://www.counterpunch.org/2009/08/28/israeli-organ-harvesting/.

Whitlock, Kay and Michael Bronski. *Considering Hate: Violence, Goodness, and Justice in American Culture and Politics*. Boston, MA: Beacon Press, 2015.

Wippermann, Wolfgang. "Politologentrug: Ideologiekritik der Extremismus-Legende" *Standpunkte*, October 2010. https://www.rosalux.de/fileadmin/rls_uploads/pdfs/Standpunkte/Standpunkte_10-2010.pdf.

Younis, Tarek. "Counter-Radicalization: A Critical Look into a Racist New Industry." *Yaqeen Institute*. 2019. https://yaqeeninstitute.org/read/paper/counter-radicalization-a-critical-look-into-a-racist-new-industry.

Younis, Tarek. *The Muslim, State and Mind: Psychology in Times of Islamophobia*. London: SAGE, 2024.

Zapotosky, Matt. "Barr Forms Task Force to Counter Anti-Government Extremists." *Washington Post*, June 26, 2020. https://www.washingtonpost.com/national-security/william-barr-task-force-anti-government-extremists-antifa-boogaloo/2020/06/26/138f424e-b7bf-11ea-a510-55bf26485c93_story.html.

CONCLUSION

From Void to Hope

Fascism has both affective and ideological components. As I have argued, *fascism is a social movement seeking power, always already connected to sources of power*, and *people have particular motivations for joining that movement, including psychological, cognitive, and emotional needs that they are seeking to fulfill through their participation.* Understanding both these dimensions is necessary for understanding how fascism operates. And understanding how fascism operates is essential for defeating it.

This book has challenged some prevailing modes of thinking about contemporary fascist movements. This has included exploring the limitations of broad categories like accelerationism and extremism, especially when these are used in ways that suggest that it is not necessary to distinguish between movements based on their ideological differences. These paradigms can be used to justify policing and securitization aimed at the left or minority populations. I have also reflected philosophically on how fascism operates, particularly the ways in which it manipulates deep human desires. I earnestly hope this work fuels fruitful discussion, debate, and praxis among those who engage these topics from a variety of angles, to contribute to work that is ethical, effective, and well-informed and that begins from a commitment to social transformation in solidarity with those most impacted by fascist and far-right harm.

Countering Fascism as a Social Movement

As a social movement, fascism must be defeated by countervailing social movements. This requires recognizing and contesting it at the heart of its connections to power, as well as at the fringes of society where its more

DOI: 10.4324/9781003031604-6

vulgar foot soldiers seek to gain ground. The influence of figures like Steve Bannon needs to be contested, and the "signaling" of affinities to fascism from those in positions of power must be watched and exposed. The "slime mold" networking style of fascism, discussed in Chapter 2, indicates that we must be aware of fascism spreading and showing up in new guises. Being attuned to fascism's deep resistance to rationality and its nature as a defense mechanism for violent filling of the void with idols helps us to see that we must look past surface statements to the underlying and symbolic expressions of dehumanization, destructiveness, and violence.

Here in my home country of the United States, many challenges present themselves. Fascism is not a problem that can be solved solely at the ballot box. Current trends suggest that we will continue to see skirmishes and violent attacks by far-right actors. Problems exist not only at the "fringe" and "extremes" but also with increasing takeover of the Republican Party by fascists. This includes watching and resisting the rise of Christian nationalism (including some fascists emphasizing or converting to Christianity in search of "tradition"), which is helping to facilitate the merger of Republican Party politics and fascist ideology. Furthermore, the spread of conspiracy theories and online far-right cultural spaces, especially under the influence of the COVID-19 pandemic, will have lasting consequences with which researchers and activists must reckon. There is increasing spread of "conspirituality," a blending of New Age spirituality and far-right conspiracy theories, which enables fascism and the far-right to penetrate new spaces like yoga studios and natural birthing communities.[1]

Resisting fascism as a social movement will also include contesting all attempts to expand its scapegoating further into the mainstream, concentrating its targeting and its "swarm"-like energies on attacking particular dehumanized groups. This will include growing intersectional solidarity and educating communities about the dynamics of dehumanization to resist its pull internally and externally. Ongoing attacks on Black and indigenous communities, LGBTQ+ individuals, and the unhoused are among the trends to watch, but targeting is ever-expanding and shifting. Furthermore, the increasing normalization of antisemitism makes fascism ever more capable of gaining ground; antisemitic conspiracy theories are often at the heart of fascist mobilization, and as more mainstream conservative politics increasingly welcomes expressions of antisemitism, fascist takeover of spaces grows.

As the climate crisis deepens, there will also be renewed appeals to revanchist nationalism, including harsh border enforcement, and eugenicist policies targeting those with disabilities and racialized minorities. The scale of the potential environmental catastrophe we are facing also endangers the vital force of hope without which revolutionary struggle is impossible. Helping one another to avoid getting stuck in numbness and shock, and to fight for human and ecological survival, will be crucial in ensuring leftist emancipatory responses predominate over ecofascism and fascist accelerationism/catastrophic messianism.

In the case of all such trends, the theory and practice of resistance must be grounded in specificity, responding to fascism in its particular manifestations as a social movement seeking power, holding particular beliefs, and operating in particular venues. Researchers and activists should seek to avoid the generalizations (like "extremism") and the neologisms (like "coalitional accelerationism" and "cumulative radicalization") that erode distinctions between fascist movements and very different social movements. In addition, our analysis and strategy must center and be in solidarity with those most impacted and those at the front lines of the struggle against fascism in their communities. Doing this also means resisting models that treat fascism as a fringe crime problem to be solved solely by law enforcement and instead embracing approaches that are connected to wider social critique and that bolster rather than undermine the long-term demands for not only the defeat of fascism but also deeper transformation and emancipation of society and the planet.

Countering Fascism's Emotional and Cognitive Pull

As I have argued, fascism is, in part, a response to a void of meaning and a sense of an abyss or absence, which plays a substantial role in recruitment into the far-right—this void must be reconfronted upon departing it. This fact suggests a need for community networks that help people face this void and work through it as a means of prevention from engagement in fascism and as a pathway out of fascism. However, prevailing practices and narratives of the "deradicalization" industry, discussed in Chapter 4, are limited, unduly burdening marginalized communities or relying on policing models, as well as often operating with a lack of credentials, murky ethical boundaries, interpersonal drama, and few to no structures of accountability to targeted communities.

Ultimately, I believe, our ability to defeat fascism will be shaped and impacted by the stories that we choose to tell, to highlight, and the stories that become dominant in our society and believed. Do we choose to believe fascism's apocalyptic narrative, according to which change comes only through a destructive period that exploits the pain of the present, as nothing but a tool for reinstituting hierarchy? Or can we embrace a revolutionary, dialectical hope that holds and builds upon the potential within the present? Do we naïvely narrate the stories of past perpetrators of violence, investing future liberation only in "compassionate" outreach by targets of hate, or do we proceed by centering the voices of those most impacted, even or especially when what they say makes those with more privilege feel uncomfortable? Those oppressed, marginalized, or targeted deserve to be heard, even if their voices never transform the hearts of haters. Radical hope resides not in crafting the right "counter-narrative" to dissuade people from fascism, but in broader societal transformation, by beginning to be what we want to become as a society.

Referencing the musical *Mary Poppins*, a friend once told me that I had helped move him a little bit away from a "put your tuppence [two-pence] in the bank" socialism toward a "feed the birds" socialism. I really quite like this analogy. In the musical, the cold and authoritarian father wants his children to become frugal bankers. He objects that they have been taught the wrong lesson when their nanny encourages the children to use their allowance to buy breadcrumbs from a poor woman to feed pigeons in the park. This simple act of connection and joy seems impractical and wasteful to him. Certainly, the left can, at times, adopt the same narrowness of thinking. But moving past capitalism is not only a question of raw power but also a question of community, values, and worldviews. As Erich Fromm would surely agree, becoming capable of new ways of organizing our society involves growth in humans' hope and transformational capacity and not only after the fact.

As the far-right will continue to appropriate tactics from the left, it becomes ever more important that the left push back by providing other structures and practices of support and engagement for wider communities, beyond mere campaigns. Mutual aid, and in Antonio Gramsci's term, structures of "dual power," will be essential. People who are desperate for help, and seeking belonging or spaces of culture engagement, joy, and exploration of ideas, need to be able to find this on the left, to make fascism's twisted and idolatrous offers less appealing. Resistance to fascism will include cultivating spaces of communal belonging and support and openness to questions of meaning. This is not only a matter of "prevention" or "intervention" against hate but also a matter of creating the kind of world we ultimately want. These approaches are only possible coupled with firm boundaries that deplatform and displace fascists at any locale on which they encroach. It is only by understanding fascism's aspects both as a social movement seeking and connected to power and as exerting a particular kind of pull on those who choose (and are responsible for that choice) to participate in it that fascism can successfully be defeated. There is a role for everyone in this work, if they are open to beginning from a position of solidarity with those most impacted. For researchers, studying the fascist threat in order to defeat it will require remaining in touch with the challenges of both theory and practice while avoiding all forms of theoretical reductivism, enabling us to be of service in the serious yet nevertheless potentially joyful and hopeful work that lies before us.

Note

1 Ward and Voas, 103.

Bibliography

Ward, Charlotte and David Voas. "The Emergence of Conspirituality." *Journal of Contemporary Religion*, 26, no. 1 (2011): 103–21.

INDEX

For Product Safety Concerns and Information please contact our EU
representative GPSR@taylorandfrancis.com
Taylor & Francis Verlag GmbH, Kaufingerstraße 24, 80331 München, Germany